# FOOTBALL
# CROSSWORDS

# FOOTBALL
# CROSSWORDS

VOLUME 3

## Dale Ratermann

MASTERS PRESS

NTC/Contemporary Publishing Group

**Library of Congress Cataloging-in-Publication Data**
is available from the United States Library of Congress.

Published by Masters Press
A division of NTC/Contemporary Publishing Group, Inc.
4255 West Touhy Avenue, Lincolnwood (Chicago), Illinois 60646-1975 U.S.A.
Copyright © 1999 by Dale Ratermann
Printed in the United States of America
International Standard Book Number: 1-57028-213-7
International Standard Serial Number: 1522-1024
99  00  01  02  03  04  VL  19  18  17  16  15  14  13  12  11  10  9  8  7  6  5  4  3  2  1

*To Debby and Jackie*

# CONTENTS

# FOOTBALL
## CROSSWORDS

# ARIZONA CARDINALS

The Cardinals' history goes back farther than any other team in the National Football League—to 1898 in the predominantly Irish area of Chicago's south side.

A neighborhood group playing for the Morgan Athletic Club competed against other amateur club teams in the Chicago area. Chris O'Brien, a painting and decorating contractor, acquired the team and in 1901 purchased used jerseys from the University of Chicago. The jerseys were a faded maroon, prompting O'Brien to say, "That's not maroon. It's cardinal red." The nickname was born.

The team disbanded in 1906 because of a lack of competition, but football was becoming more popular in 1913 and O'Brien reorganized the team. By 1917 the Cardinals had new uniforms and hired their first coach, Marshall Smith. They were the champions of the Chicago Football League that year.

A flu epidemic and World War I forced the team to suspend operations again in 1918, but at the end of the war, the team returned. The "Racine Cardinals" (named for a street in Chicago) became one of the 11 charter members of the American Professional Football League, which in 1920 evolved into the NFL. The franchise fee was $100.

After joining the league and stepping up a level in competition, O'Brien had to find more good players. He signed Northwestern University halfback "Paddy" Driscoll to a $3,000 contract, the richest at the time. Driscoll was a superstar and the finest drop kicker in history.

The Cardinals were 6–2 in their first year in the league, then 3–3–2 in 1921. The following season a team from Racine, Wis., joined the NFL, forcing the Cardinals to change their name to "Chicago Cardinals." The Cardinals won their first championship in 1925 under new coach Norman Barry.

On Thanksgiving Day in 1929, one of the greatest individual performances in league history took place in a Cardinals' game. Ernie Nevers, coaxed out of retirement to become a player/coach at the age of 26, scored 40 points on six touchdowns and four extra points to lead the Cardinals to a 40–6 victory over the cross-town Chicago Bears.

In the 1930s the Cardinals were the league's doormat and were hit hard by the effects of World War II. They were forced to join with the Pittsburgh Steelers to form a team in 1944. Still, the Chicago/Pittsburgh team went 0–10.

Following the war, the Cardinals put together the "million-dollar backfield" featuring quarterback Paul Christman, fullback Pat Harder, halfback Elmer Angsman and halfback Charley Trippi. The Cardinals won the 1947 Western Division title with a 9–3 record and beat the Philadelphia Eagles, 28–21, in the NFL championship game. The Cardinals reached the title game again the following year, but lost the rematch with Philadelphia, 7–0.

The Cardinals struggled through the 1950s. They did have a highlight of note in 1959, scoring five touchdowns on punt returns, still an NFL record.

Unable to compete with the Bears in Chicago, the franchise finally moved to St. Louis prior to the 1960 campaign. It took 14 years in the new city for the Cardinals to win another division title. Safety Larry Wilson, one of the greatest players in the franchise's history, retired after the 1972 season, but the Cardinals still had players such as quarterback Jim Hart, running back Terry Metcalf, cornerback Roger Wehrli, offensive tackles Ernie McMillan and Dan Dierdorf, kicker Jim Bakken and tight end Jackie Smith. Under the direction of coach Don Coryell, the Cardinals won the NFC Eastern Division in 1974 with a 10–4 record. They lost to Minnesota, 30–14, in the first round of the playoffs.

The Cardinals won the division again in 1975 (11–3) and lost in the first round of the playoffs to the Los Angeles Rams, 35–23. Coryell left following the 1977 season. The Cardinals were back in the playoffs with a 5–4 record in the strike-shortened season of 1982, but lost in the first round again, to Green Bay, 41–16.

After 28 years in St. Louis, the Cardinals moved to Arizona prior to the 1988 season. The Cardinals were 7–9 in their first season as the "Phoenix Cardinals," but set club records for largest single-game attendance (67,139) and largest season attendance (472,937).

They have failed to improve on that seasonal mark. Most of the blame can go to the team's performance on the field. It has yet to have a winning record.

Joe Bugel became the head coach in 1990, and the team produced records of 5–11, 4–12, 4–12 and 7–9. Following the 1993 season, the franchise made a couple of changes: its name became "Arizona Cardinals," and the controversial Buddy Ryan was named head coach.

Ryan lasted just two seasons—winning a total of 12 games. He was replaced by Vince Tobin prior to the 1996 campaign. The Cardinals were 7–9 in 1996 and 4–12 in '97.

The franchise has been owned by the Bidwell family since 1932, when Charles Bidwell, Sr., a vice president of the Chicago Bears, purchased the Cardinals for $50,000 and left the Bears. Charles ran the club until his death in the 1947 championship season. His wife, Violet, guided the team for 15 years, then passed the franchise to their two sons, William and Charles, Jr. William became the sole owner in 1972.

*Leland McElroy led the Cardinals in rushing in 1997.*

## INDIVIDUAL RECORDS

### Career

Rushing Yards: 7,999, Ottis Anderson, 1979–86

Passing Yards: 34,639, Jim Hart, 1966–83

Receptions: 522, Roy Green, 1979–90

Interceptions: 52, Larry Wilson, 1960–72

Touchdowns: 70, Roy Green, 1979–90

Points: 1,380, Jim Bakken, 1962–78

### Season

Rushing Yards: 1,605, Ottis Anderson, 1979

Passing Yards: 4,614, Neil Lomax, 1984

Receptions: 101, Larry Centers, 1995

Interceptions: 12, Bob Nussbaumer, 1949

Touchdowns: 17, John David Crow, 1962

Points: 117, Jim Bakken, 1967, and Neil O'Donoghue, 1984

## ACROSS

3. CB Aeneas or WR Kevin
8. Cardinals' career scoring leader
10. Up and ___
11. WR
13. BYU DT Shawn ___
14. Makes a sharp turn
15. 1st non-college draftee since '46
16. Covers the TE
18. Holiday that cost Arizona its original Super Bowl date (init.)
19. Johnny McWilliams' alma mater (init.)
21. Cardinals' career receiving leader

23. Retain
26. Has
27. Rush
30. Down and ___
33. Former home of the Cardinals
35. Short yardage play
37. Stadium signage
38. Cardinals' career passing leader
41. Expected touch down for charter (init.)
42. Squad
43. Threw for team record 4,614 yards in '84
44. Against (abbr.)
45. HB

46. 3 ___ in a yard
47. Cardinals' career rushing leader
49. ___ mask
50. Period of time
51. Try (abbr.)
52. Defeat
55. Possible starting time of game
56. Qtr.
57. Thrown out
59. There are 120 on a field (abbr.)
61. Ankle wrap
62. Where severely injured players are sent (init.)
63. 1 of 3 or more
64. Set team rushing record with 214 yards in '96 game
67. Led Cardinals in receiving in '97
68. Team physician (abbr.)
69. ___ back passer

**DOWN**

1. ___-announcer (init.)
2. Set team record with 101 catches in '95
3. Cardinals' career interceptions leader was head coach for 3 games
4. Middle defender (init.)
5. Super agent ___ Tellem
6. Stadium advertisements
7. Blocks
8. Esiason
9. Boot
12. After quarter, half or full
13. Leg joint

17. Football/baseball star from Auburn (not Bo)
20. ___-captain
22. Cardinals' division
24. Evan Arapostathis' alma mater (init.)
25. Column heading on roster (abbr.)
28. Without a loss
29. Jake
31. 6-pointer (abbr.)
32. Diagrams
34. 1-on-1 (abbr.)
36. List for hurt players (init.)
39. Beyond RG
40. Shoulder, hip or knee
43. Get beaten
44. Win
47. Yards gained divided by carries
48. Scored NFL record 40 points in '29 game
49. Spectator
52. Wager
53. Ball prop
54. Goose egg
58. Yards needed for a 1st down
59. Column heading on roster (abbr.)
60. Capacity crowd (init.)
63. 1st ___ 10
64. College class of early entry (abbr.)
65. ___ and WT
66. Wire service (init.)

*Solution on page 182*

**RETIRED UNIFORM NUMBERS**

Larry Wilson—8

Stan Mauldin—77

J. V. Cain—88

Marshall Goldberg—99

```
E  P  R  A  H  S  E  D  L  A  N  O  D  C  M
A  S  O  M  C  M  I  L  L  A  N  L  S  D  R
T  R  A  H  O  A  R  A  H  N  A  W  O  I  E
I  E  E  S  M  I  T  H  N  T  A  P  L  E  M
S  T  C  A  A  L  J  O  H  N  S  O  N  R  M
C  N  F  R  G  L  D  I  N  N  D  R  C  D  U
O  E  C  Y  O  I  H  O  E  W  P  V  H  O  L
S  C  N  E  V  W  S  E  B  K  O  U  A  R  P
S  M  N  E  S  E  R  M  A  L  I  R  R  F  W
N  O  S  R  E  D  N  A  K  N  E  I  B  S  E
O  K  U  L  L  R  H  O  K  A  C  R  T  X  H
S  R  C  R  C  O  G  G  E  E  L  E  Y  W  R
L  O  T  M  A  T  S  O  N  D  E  R  C  E  L
I  R  A  N  D  L  E  E  N  E  V  E  R  S  I
W  F  N  R  E  X  A  M  O  L  I  M  M  X  C
```

| | | |
|---|---|---|
| ANDERSON | HART | RANDLE |
| BAKKEN | JOHNSON | RICE |
| BROWN | LOMAX | SHARPE |
| CENTERS | MATSON | SMITH |
| CROW | MCDONALD | SWANN |
| DIERDORF | MCMILLAN | WEHRLI |
| DOBLER | NEVERS | WILLIAMS |
| GREEN | PLUMMER | WILSON |

# ATLANTA FALCONS

**T**he Atlanta Falcons were the 15th National Football League team, joining the league as an expansion franchise for the 1966 season. Rankin M. Smith, of the Life Insurance Company of Georgia, paid $8.5 million for the franchise. In a 54-day period prior to the season, the Falcons sold 45,000 season tickets, surpassing the previous NFL best by nearly 20,000.

As the newest team, Atlanta got the No. 1 pick in the college draft prior to its inaugural season. The Falcons selected Tommy Nobis, the Outland Trophy-winning linebacker from the University of Texas. Nobis also was picked by the Houston Oilers of the American Football League, but he chose the Falcons and on Dec. 14, 1965, signed a contract. In all, the Falcons drafted 25 players in the 20-round draft.

Atlanta also was able to select three backup players off each of the other 14 teams. Among those picked in the expansion draft were the Falcons' first rushing leader, Junior Coffey from the Green Bay Packers, their first receiving leader, Alex Hawkins from the Baltimore Colts, and their first defensive captain, Bill Jabko from the Minnesota Vikings.

Norb Hecker was the club's first coach. He had been an assistant for Vince Lombardi at Green Bay while the Packers were winning three world titles and four conference championships.

The Falcons lost their first game, 19–14, at home against the Los Angeles Rams, and didn't get their first win—a 27–16 victory over the New York Giants—until the 10th game of the season. They won three of their final five games to finish 3–11, tying an NFL record for most wins by an expansion team. Individually, the brightest spot was Nobis, who earned NFL Rookie of the Year honors.

The Falcons won only one game in 1967, however, and got off to an 0–3 start the following season. Hecker was replaced by Norm Van Brocklin, but the team won just two of its remaining 11 games to finish 2–12.

The Falcons made a major stride forward in 1969 when they finished 6–8 behind quarterback Bob Berry and running back Jim "Cannonball" Butler. They snapped Minnesota's 12-game winning streak with a 10–3 win in the season finale. The game's only touchdown was scored by defensive end Claude Humphrey (who played in six Pro Bowls) on a 24-yard fumble return.

The Falcons struggled in 1970 (4–8–2) and won seven games each in 1971 and '72. They went 9–5 in 1973, with a seven-game winning streak, but missed a playoff spot by just one game. However, when they started 2–6 in 1974, Van

Brocklin was replaced by defensive coordinator Marion Campbell. The Falcons finished the year 3–11. After that season, the Falcons traded Pro Bowl offensive tackle George Kunz and a draft choice to the Baltimore Colts in exchange for the No. 1 pick in the 1975 college draft. Atlanta used that selection to draft the University of California's all-America quarterback Steve Bartkowski.

With Bartkowski starting, the Falcons went 4–10 in 1975. Dave Hampton, who had come close the previous two years, became the club's first 1,000-yard rusher that season. The Falcons started 1–4 in 1976, Campbell was let go, and general manager Pat Peppler completed the 4–10 season as the interim coach.

Prior to the 1977 season, former NFL quarterback Eddie LeBaron was named the general manager. Two days later he named Leeman Bennett the new head coach. The Falcons improved to 7–7 and second place in the Western Division, then qualified for their first playoffs with a 9–7 record the following year. As a Wild Card team, the Falcons hosted the Philadelphia Eagles on Christmas Eve. The Falcons scored two touchdowns in the final eight minutes and survived rainy weather and a missed 34–yard field goal attempt by the Eagles in the final seconds for a 14–13 win.

The following week they were 14-point underdogs to the Dallas Cowboys. They jumped to a 20–13 halftime lead and knocked Dallas quarterback Roger Staubach unconscious just before the half, but the Cowboys rallied in the second half and won, 27–20. The Falcons had a chance to tie the game late, but failed on a fourth-down-and-one at the Cowboy 32-yard line in the final minute.

Atlanta slipped to 6–10 in 1979, but returned to the playoffs the following year as the Western Division champions. Bartkowski threw for 3,544 yards and William Andrews rushed for 1,308 yards as the team finished 12–4. The playoffs brought more disappointment, however. The Falcons entered the final quarter of their first-round game against Dallas with a 24–10 lead, but the Cowboys scored 20 fourth-quarter points to win, 30–27.

The Falcons slid to a 7–9 record in 1981 and were 5–4 in the strike-shortened 1982 season. That was the last time they finished .500 or better until 1991. That season, young players such as quarterback Chris Miller, wide receivers Andre Rison and Michael Haynes and defensive back Deion Sanders rallied around coach Jerry Glanville and won five of their last six games to go 10–6. That was good enough for a Wild Card spot in the playoffs. The Falcons beat the Saints in New Orleans, 27–20, then lost to the Redskins in Washington, 24–7.

The Falcons slipped to 6–10 in 1992 and '93, and changes were in store. Glanville was replaced as head coach by offensive coordinator June Jones, and quarterback Jeff George was acquired from the Indianapolis Colts.

Atlanta was 7–9 in 1994, then qualified for the playoffs with a 9–7 mark in '95. The Falcons were beaten by the Green Bay Packers, 37–20, in a Wild Card game.

During the 1996 season, George was suspended by the team for four games following a much-publicized spat with Jones. The Falcons finished the year 3–13, then released George.

In 1997 the Falcons rallied by winning five of their final six games to finish 7–9, but it wasn't enough to save Jones his job. He was replaced by Dan Reeves, the NFL's winningest active coach.

*Byron Hanspard rushed for 335 yards in 1997, his rookie season.*

## INDIVIDUAL RECORDS
### Career

Rushing Yards:  6,631, Gerald Riggs, 1982–88

Passing Yards:  23,468, Steve Bartkowski, 1975–85

Receptions:  423, Andre Rison, 1990–94

Interceptions:  39, Rolland Lawrence, 1973–80

Touchdowns:  56, Andre Rison, 1990–94

Points:  558, Mick Luckhurst, 1981–87

### Season

Rushing Yards:  1,719, Gerald Riggs, 1985

Passing Yards:  4,143, Jeff George, 1995

Receptions:  111, Terance Mathis, 1994

Interceptions:  10, Scott Case, 1988

Touchdowns:  15, Andre Rison, 1993

Points:  122, Morten Andersen, 1995

## ACROSS

1. MNF network
2. Applaud
6. Stadium signage
7. Unit with the ball (abbr.)
10. 1/3 of a yard
12. QB: ___ caller
13. Had 104 catches in '95
15. Lineman
18. Easy
20. ___-announcer (init.)
21. Ball prop
23. Stop in play (abbr.)
24. Move or turn away from the line
26. Falcons' career interceptions leader
28. Point value of PAT kick
29. Column heading on roster (abbr.)
31. Championship
33. ___ Super Bowl
34. Falcons' career rushing leader
37. Stumble
38. Threw for team record 416 yards in '81 game
40. ___ Cappelletti
42. Belonging to us
44. 6-pointers (abbr.)
45. Scored team record 122 points in '95

48. Leg joint
51. NFC West rival (init.)
52. Threw for team record 4,143 yards in '95
53. Locker room snappers
56. Value of PAT run into the end zone
57. Lou "The ___" Groza
58. Against (abbr.)
61. Falcons' leading receiver was a QB at Rice
63. Ball snappers
64. Down and ___

## DOWN

1. Aide
3. Head protection
4. Division name
5. Billy Joe
6. Try (abbr.)
8. QB traded to Green Bay
9. Hike
11. Todd Kinchen's alma mater (init.)
14. ___-captain
15. Wall opening
16. Away
17. Guard
19. Maybe
22. Had team record 111 catches in '94
25. Keep your ___ on the ball
27. Block from behind
30. Middle defensive lineman (init.)
32. Not on time
34. Falcons' career receiving leader
35. DE led '97 team with 12 QB sacks
36. Had 6 FG in '94 game
37. 7–7 and 21–21
39. Had team-record 15 catches in '81 game
41. Foe
43. Official
46. Falcons' coach in '97
47. Dine
49. Up and ___
50. 3-pointer (init.)
54. Possess
55. ___ Louis
56. Video monitors (abbr.)
59. Travis Hall's position (init.)
60. Play ___ or trade me!
62. Stomach muscle (abbr.)

*Solution on page 182*

## RETIRED UNIFORM NUMBERS

Steve Bartkowski—10

William Andrews—31

Jeff Van Note—57

Tommy Nobis—60

```
D  L  E  A  H  P  E  L  G  G  U  T  E  R  B
I  S  F  R  A  L  I  C  A  U  S  L  P  E  U
M  A  I  R  I  N  S  N  I  K  N  E  J  E  T
I  A  O  B  O  S  N  Y  A  D  D  I  D  E  L
T  P  E  A  O  F  O  H  R  N  C  N  O  A  E
C  R  T  R  J  N  F  N  R  O  H  R  H  R
H  A  O  Y  E  L  L  E  H  S  U  I  S  U  N
E  O  N  T  G  M  K  Z  N  G  G  C  E  M  A
L  M  N  E  E  O  U  H  U  G  N  C  V  P  Y
L  B  A  R  T  K  O  W  S  K  I  B  A  H  R
D  V  V  G  J  J  K  A  A  N  I  Z  E  R  B
A  E  A  A  O  E  A  O  L  K  Y  C  R  E  Z
Z  N  M  T  S  R  U  H  K  C  U  L  A  Y  O
N  E  L  A  N  T  I  V  C  A  T  Y  O  S  G
S  A  L  A  U  A  N  D  R  E  W  S  B  I  E
```

| | | |
|---|---|---|
| ANDREWS | GANN | NOBIS |
| BARTKOWSKI | HUMPHREY | RADE |
| BREZINA | JAMES | REAVES |
| BRYAN | JENKINS | RIGGS |
| BUTLER | JOHNSON | RISON |
| CASE | KENN | SHELLEY |
| CURRY | LUCKHURST | TUGGLE |
| FRALIC | MITCHELL | VAN NOTE |

# BALTIMORE RAVENS

**T**he city of Baltimore gained one football team, but lost the history of two other franchises.

The Baltimore Colts began in 1946 in the All-America Football Conference, relocating to Maryland from Miami. Following the 1949 season, the Colts and two other AAFC teams merged into the National Football League. The Baltimore Colts won NFL championships in 1958, '59, '68 and '70. However, on a spring night in 1984, owner Robert Irsay loaded the Colts' possessions into Mayflower vans and moved the team to Indianapolis. With it went the four championship trophies, Johnny Unitas' 39,768 passing yards, Lydell Mitchell's 5,487 rushing yards, Raymond Berry's 631 pass receptions and the blue horseshoe logo on the side of white helmets.

The city went without NFL football until Art Modell moved his Cleveland Browns franchise to Baltimore on Feb. 9, 1996. But did he? Sure, moving to Baltimore was Cleveland quarterback Vinny Testaverde, and No. 38 in the defensive backfield certainly looked like the Browns' Antonio Langham. In reality, the NFL required Modell to leave the Browns nickname, team colors and history with the city of Cleveland. No Jim Brown, Paul Warfield, Leroy Kelly, Otto Graham, Lou Groza or Paul Brown. No Dr. Frank Ryan, Bernie Kosar or Ozzie Newsome. No titles to brag about. And no entries in the team records book.

So, what did Baltimore get? It got an owner with 35 years of football experience, a team of players coming off a 5–11 season, and the return to big-time football.

The city is thankful to Modell, the same man who is considered a demon in Cleveland for moving the franchise out of town. Modell purchased the Browns in 1961 at the age of 35 for what was then an unheard of sum of $4 million. How he got in position to own a football team is amazing. He dropped out of high school to help support his family after the death of his father. His first full-time job was as an electrician's helper, cleaning out the hulls of ships in a Brooklyn shipyard. After a stint in the Air Force, he enrolled in a New York television school. He produced one of the first regular daytime TV shows in the nation, then entered the advertising business in 1954.

Since joining the NFL, Modell has been the league president and chairman of the television, owner's labor and merger committees. He also is chairman of NFL Films. He was instrumental in ABC's start of Monday Night Football and staged the first doubleheader in NFL history in the 1962 preseason. He also serves on the board of Churchill Downs, the Cleveland Clinic, Baldwin Wallace College and Cleveland State University. His wife, Pat Modell, is one of the most recognized actresses in television history. At one point, she had appeared in more motion pictures and TV shows (400) than any other actress. She was a regular on *People's Choice* and *General Hospital.*

The "new" franchise in Baltimore came up with a new name: the "Ravens." It got new colors: black, purple and metallic gold. It got (sort of) a new coach: Ted Marchibroda. Marchibroda coached the Baltimore Colts from 1975–79 and the Indianapolis Colts from 1992–95. And they got construction started on a new stadium, scheduled to open for the 1998 season.

With their first-ever draft choice, the Ravens selected UCLA offensive lineman Jonathan Ogden (fourth overall pick). They added another first-rounder (26th overall) in University of Miami linebacker Ray Lewis.

It didn't take Baltimore long to fall in love with football again. The Ravens sold more than 50,000 season tickets in 14 days. Their opening game, Sept. 1, 1996, was played in front of 64,124 fans at Memorial Stadium, the largest crowd in Baltimore's professional sports history. The Ravens pleased the fans by winning, 19–14, over the Oakland Raiders.

The first Ravens squad finished 4–12. It was 4–4 at home and 0–8 on the road. There were 10 sellouts (including two preseason games). The Ravens held a second-half lead in 10 of its final 11 games, but won only two. The highlights included Testaverde throwing for 4,177 yards and 33 touchdowns. He was voted to the Pro Bowl. Wide receivers Michael Jackson and Derrick Alexander both exceeded 1,000 yards in pass receptions and combined for 23 touchdowns. Bam Morris led the team in rushing with 737 yards; Earnest Byner added 634 yards.

In 1997 the Ravens won three of their first four games, beating the Cincinnati Bengals, New York Giants and Tennessee Oilers. They also won two of their last three games, downing the Seattle Seahawks and Oilers. However, in-between, they were just 1–7–1 (beating the Washington Redskins and tying the Philadelphia Eagles). The 6–9–1 finish left them in last place in the American Football Conference's Central Division.

Testaverde again led the offense, completing 57.7 percent of his passes for 2,971 yards and 18 TDs. Morris again led the team in rushing with 774 yards. Alexander surpassed 1,000 yards (1,009) receiving for the second straight year, but Jackson fell just short (918). Peter Boulware had 11.5 quarterback sacks; Stevon Moore had four interceptions.

In the 1998 college draft, the Ravens selected cornerback Duane Starks from the University of Miami with the 10th overall pick in the first round.

*Tackle Jonathan Ogden was the first player ever selected by the Ravens in the college draft.*

## INDIVIDUAL RECORDS

### Career

Rushing Yards: 1,511, Bam Morris, 1996–97

Passing Yards: 7,148, Vinny Testaverde, 1996–97

Receptions: 145, Michael Jackson, 1996–97

Interceptions: 8, Antonio Langham, 1996–97

Touchdowns: 18, Michael Jackson, 1996–97, and Derrick Alexander, 1996–97

Points: 201, Matt Stover, 1996–97

### Season

Rushing Yards: 774, Bam Morris, 1997

Passing Yards: 4,177, Vinny Testaverde, 1996

Receptions: 76, Michael Jackson, 1996

Interceptions: 5, Antonio Langham, 1996, and Eric Turner, 1996

Touchdowns: 14, Michael Jackson, 1996

Points: 110, Matt Stover, 1997

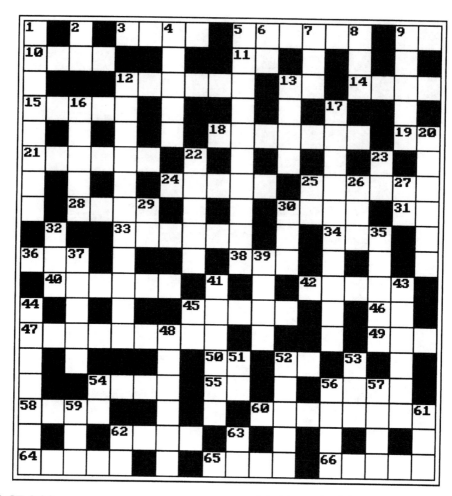

## ACROSS

3. Remaining
5. Championship hardware
9. ___-captain
10. Division name
11. Baltimore's time zone (init.)
12. Bam
13. On the back of a jersey (abbr.)
14. Slide away
15. PAT: ___ point
18. Ravens' career receiving leader
19. Usual college class of draftees (abbr.)
21. Body position prior to snap
24. Has rushed for more than 8,000 career yards
25. Begins the game
28. Sign on stadium gate
30. Limbs
31. Extra period (abbr.)
33. Scorched
34. Down and ___
36. Block
38. Dine
40. Tosses
42. Ravens' kick return specialist
45. ___ of game penalty
46. ___ Louis

47. Had more than 1,000 yards receiving two straight seasons
49. Lou "The ___" Groza
50. Down and ___
52. AFC foe (init.)
54. Not covered
55. Orlando Brown's position (init.)
56. Hall of ___
58. ___ mark
60. Rookie LB had team-leading 11.5 sacks in '97
62. 3–3 and 10–10
64. Led team with 4 interceptions in '97
65. Get beaten
66. Bottom half of uniform

## DOWN

1. 4–3, 3–4 and Prevent
2. ___ vs. Them
4. ___ and 10
5. Vinny
6. Outside of RG
7. Paid player
8. Do the Ravens have a marching band?
9. Blocks from behind
12. Ravens' head coach
13. Shoe giant
16. Swap
17. Ravens' punter
20. List of players

22. Knotting the score
23. Run back fourth-down boot (init.)
25. WR
26. Richard Mann's alma mater (init.)
27. Go ___ guy
29. Jack Bravyak's alma mater (init.)
30. Back muscle (abbr.)
32. Rest on the bench
35. Spin
37. Point value of FG
39. At
41. Quarter
43. Ravens' kicker has career best 55-yd. FG
44. Ravens' career interceptions leader
45. Michael McCrary's position (init.)
48. Former Colt had 3 INT in '97
51. Middle defensive lineman (init.)
52. Get 6 points
53. Rule
54. 1st word in the national anthem
56. Toss
57. Primary
59. Capacity crowd (init.)
61. Sutter, et al.
62. Brian Kinchen's position (init.)
63. ___ or die

*Solution on page 183*

---

**RETIRED UNIFORM NUMBERS**

None

```
M  W  S  T  A  D  O  R  B  I  H  C  R  A  M
O  C  T  U  L  L  E  W  D  L  A  C  R  H  T
N  I  C  V  E  N  E  M  E  N  R  I  G  U  E
T  T  L  R  X  G  I  O  E  T  G  I  R  X  S
G  X  E  A  A  T  S  D  E  H  E  N  A  S  T
O  O  W  X  N  R  G  I  B  P  E  H  H  T  A
M  R  I  I  D  O  Y  Z  L  R  I  E  A  O  V
E  D  S  Z  E  N  E  D  A  G  O  I  M  V  E
R  V  R  L  R  I  N  A  S  R  N  W  S  E  R
Y  U  J  A  E  M  O  N  Y  T  I  E  N  R  D
R  K  U  R  O  S  S  I  Z  A  N  L  E  U  E
A  R  N  R  O  H  K  E  I  O  G  E  L  R  L
H  O  R  N  O  W  C  L  J  M  O  O  R  E  G
A  I  T  R  S  D  A  E  R  A  W  L  U  O  B
S  R  E  N  Y  B  J  K  I  N  C  H  E  N  R
```

| | | |
|---|---|---|
| ALEXANDER | HOARD | MOORE |
| BOULWARE | JACKSON | MORRIS |
| BROWN | JONES | OGDEN |
| BYNER | KINCHEN | ROE |
| CALDWELL | LEWIS | STOVER |
| DANIEL | MARCHIBRODA | TESTAVERDE |
| GRAHAM | MCCRARY | TURNER |
| GREEN | MONTGOMERY | ZEIER |

# BUFFALO BILLS

**F**our Super Bowls in a row. A feat no team in the history of the National Football League has matched. Time for celebration, right?

Wrong, if you're a runner-up each time. Buffalo won the American Football Conference title and advanced to the Super Bowl following the 1990, '91, '92 and '93 seasons, but lost the championship game all four times.

In 1993, the Bills coasted to a 12–4 record and a bye in the first round of the playoffs. Then they beat the Los Angeles Raiders and Kansas City Chiefs to set up a rematch in Super Bowl XXVIII against the Dallas Cowboys. The Bills lost, 30–13.

The 1992 playoffs began on a most promising note for the Bills, who finished the regular season with an 11–5 record. They trailed the Houston Oilers, 35–3, early in the third quarter of their first-round game, but rallied for a 41–38 overtime victory—the greatest comeback in NFL history.

The Bills then beat the Pittsburgh Steelers and Miami Dolphins to set up their appearance against Dallas in Super Bowl XXVII. Buffalo scored first for a 7–0 lead, but quickly committed two turnovers that led to Dallas touchdowns. The Bills finished the game with nine turnovers, a Super Bowl record, and lost, 52–17.

Buffalo finished the 1991 regular season with a 13–3 record. The Bills beat Kansas City and the Denver Broncos in the playoffs and faced the Washington Redskins in Super Bowl XXVI. The Redskins built a 24–0 lead and won, 37–24.

The Bills also finished 13–3 in 1990. They eliminated Miami and the L.A. Raiders in the playoffs and faced the New York Giants in Super Bowl XXV. In a game whose importance was magnified by the ongoing Gulf War, Buffalo's Scott Norwood was wide right on a 47-yard field goal attempt in the final seconds, and the Giants won, 20–19.

Four seasons of hard work and success. However, the bottom line was the Super Bowl scoreboard.

The city of Buffalo was home for a number of professional football teams before the Bills arrived. As early as 1920, the All-Americans were part of the old American Football League, then joined what would become the NFL in 1921. Future teams were called the Bisons (three times), Rangers, Indians and Tigers. The Bills played in the All-America Football Conference from 1947–49, then resurfaced in 1960 in the latest American Football League.

The first AFL team, under coach Garrard "Buster" Ramsey, finished 5–8–1. The Bills were 6–8 the following year, but Ramsey was fired and replaced by Lou Saban. Led by fullback Cookie Gilchrist's league-leading 1,096 yards, the Bills had their first winning season in 1962 at 7–6–1. The next year, Buffalo tied for a division title and made the playoffs for the first time. Gilchrist was again the star, rushing for an all-time pro record (since broken) of 243 yards and five touchdowns in one game. Jack Kemp (who later became better known as a politician) was the starting quarterback that season and held the job for six years.

Saban was the Coach of the Year in 1964, when the Bills finished with a league-best 12–2 record. In the AFL championship game, Gilchrist rushed for 122 yards as the Bills beat the San Diego Chargers, 20–7, for their first title.

The Bills repeated in 1965 as Kemp was named MVP. They shut out San Diego in the title game, 23–0. Buffalo hasn't won a championship since.

Saban resigned prior to the 1966 season and was replaced by Joe Collier. Collier guided the Bills to another Eastern Division title, but they lost to Kansas City, 31–7, in the championship game (and the right to play in the first Super Bowl). In 1970, the Bills (and nine other AFL teams) merged into the NFL.

The Bills didn't have a winning record again until 1973. With Saban back as coach, O. J. Simpson rushed for a then-record 2,003 yards. The Bills went 9–5 in 1974 and qualified for the NFL playoffs for the first time, but lost to the Pittsburgh Steelers, 32–14.

Simpson continued his assault on the records book in 1975 with 23 touchdowns (since broken), but the Bills slid to 8–6 and out of the playoffs. Saban quit in mid-season of 1976, and the Bills dropped to 2–12. Prior to the 1978 season, Simpson was traded to the San Francisco 49ers. "The Juice" had rushed for 10,183 yards and scored 70 touchdowns in his nine seasons in Buffalo. In 1985 he became the first Bill inducted into the Pro Football Hall of Fame.

The Bills struggled until 1980 when they won the Eastern Division title with an 11–5 record. They lost in the first round of the playoffs to San Diego, 20–14, but were back in postseason play the following year after going 10–6. This time they beat the New York Jets, 31–27, but lost to the Cincinnati Bengals, 28–21. The Bills hit another lull and didn't surface again until two valuable acquisitions in 1986. Quarterback Jim Kelly was signed out of the United States Football League and Marv Levy was named the head coach midway through the season.

The Bills won the first of five straight division titles with a league-best 12–4 record in 1988. They lost in the AFC championship game that year and lost in the first round of the playoffs in 1989. However, 1990 began their string of four straight Super Bowls.

Kelly retired following the 1996 season. He spent 11 years in Buffalo and threw for 35,467 yards and 237 touchdowns.

Levy retired after the Bills finished 6–10 in 1997. His Buffalo teams won 123 games and lost 78. They made eight playoff appearances in 12 seasons. He was replaced by Wade Phillips, the Bills' defensive coordinator the last three years.

*Copyright © 1996 Brian Spurlock/Spurlock Photography, Inc.*

*Bruce Smith has 154 quarterback sacks in 13 seasons.*

## INDIVIDUAL RECORDS

### Career

Rushing Yards: 11,405, Thurman Thomas, 1988–97

Passing Yards: 35,467, Jim Kelly, 1986–96

Receptions: 826, Andre Reed, 1985–97

Interceptions: 40, Butch Byrd, 1964–70

Touchdowns: 83, Thurman Thomas, 1988–97

Points: 670, Scott Norwood, 1985–91

### Season

Rushing Yards: 2,003, O. J. Simpson, 1973

Passing Yards: 3,844, Jim Kelly, 1991

Receptions: 90, Andre Reed, 1994

Interceptions: 10, Billy Atkins, 1961, and Tom Janik, 1967

Touchdowns: 23, O. J. Simpson, 1975

Points: 138, O. J. Simpson, 1975

## ACROSS

2. Dubbed the greatest special teams player of all time
6. Game spheres
9. Type of x-ray (init.)
10. Kickoff return team
12. Bills' career rushing leader
15. 7–7
16. Deflect a FGA (init.)
17. Contest
18. 2-sport star Jackson
19. 6-pointers (abbr.)
22. Virginia Techer was 1st player chosen in the '85 draft
23. ___ Angeles
25. Former
26. Opening play of the game (abbr.)
27. ___-captain
28. Threw for team-record 419 yards in '83 game
31. ___ of game
32. ___ Louis
34. Treatment for sprained ankle
35. Outside of LG
36. Bills' coach, 1978–82
37. Lowly substitute
38. Bills' winningest coach
40. Not covered
41. Designate

44. Possible maker of replay screen
45. Sums
47. Pick off (abbr.)
49. Moisture collector
50. Arm joints
51. ___ Parseghian
52. Ducat
56. Column heading on roster
58. Iowa WR Quinn ___
59. Leaps
61. Stop in play (init.)
62. Straying from proper course
63. There are 120 of them on a field
64. Former competitive pro league (init.)

## DOWN

1. Covers like a blanket
2. Championship
3. Former QB turned politician
4. Cap
5. Fruit drink
7. Query
8. Ahead
11. Time of day under the lights
13. Column heading on roster (abbr.)
14. The Juice
16. Crowd cheer of displeasure
18. One of Bills' team colors
20. Display time and which team is ahead
21. Go ___ it!
24. Body position before the snap
26. Bills' career passing leader
29. A cheer
30. Richmond DB Jeff ___
31. Unit without the ball
33. Tendency
39. Aide
42. ___ to guy
43. Swatted
44. Study the key
45. Yards received divided by catches
46. Halt
48. LB was 2-time all-pro pick in the '90s
49. Usual college game day (abbr.)
53. Makes a sharp turn
54. Deflects
55. Part of a foot
57. Hole in side of a helmet
60. Publicity (init.)

*Solution on page 183*

**RETIRED UNIFORM NUMBERS**

None

```
U  I  S  A  L  R  E  M  S  T  T  C  F  S  W
V  T  A  U  S  A  M  O  H  T  A  H  R  R  E
Y  A  A  K  E  L  L  Y  E  R  D  R  O  E  R
K  A  C  S  C  R  G  N  A  T  S  I  O  B  U
T  K  O  A  K  A  N  Z  G  E  S  S  O  R  E
S  E  L  R  N  E  E  B  N  E  N  T  W  A  L
I  M  L  Y  B  B  R  O  W  N  R  I  B  B  L
R  P  I  E  N  Y  J  S  M  B  U  E  R  E  E
H  O  N  I  W  A  Z  O  M  S  Y  N  C  S  I
C  S  S  E  Z  W  J  N  H  I  O  R  I  T  M
L  L  R  L  D  A  L  A  O  S  T  L  D  E  A
I  E  U  E  M  N  W  E  P  R  L  H  W  R  L
G  N  E  E  I  U  C  M  V  L  A  L  N  O  E
H  R  S  W  S  D  I  R  U  Y  D  A  T  S  D
S  A  I  M  E  S  S  H  D  R  O  F  L  O  W
```

| | | |
|---|---|---|
| BARBER | GILCHRIST | SAIMES |
| BENNETT | HULL | SHAW |
| BROWN | JAMES | SIMPSON |
| BYRD | JONES | SMERLAS |
| CHRISTIE | KELLY | SMITH |
| COLLINS | KEMP | TASKER |
| DELAMIELLEURE | LEVY | THOMAS |
| DUNAWAY | REED | WOLFORD |

# CAROLINA PANTHERS

It was a long time coming, but well worth the wait. On Apr. 16, 1987, Jerry Richardson approached NationsBank Chairman Hugh McColl about the idea of getting a National Football League team for the Carolinas. A lot of lobbying, a lot of fund raising and a lot of answered prayers eventually brought the announcement on Oct. 26, 1993 that the NFL was awarding the 29th franchise to Charlotte, N.C. It was dubbed the "Carolina Panthers."

The work did not let up. With a new stadium being built, but not completed in time for the team's first season, Clemson University's Memorial Stadium was selected as the home field. Mike McCormack, a Hall of Fame lineman with the Cleveland Browns and former president, general manager and head coach of the Seattle Seahawks was named the president; Bill Polian was selected the general manager.

In the fall of 1994, the Panthers signed their first free agents, despite not having a coaching staff in place. Joining the Panthers were Matt Campbell, Randy Cuthbert, Kevin Farkas, Mike Finn, Willie Green, Carlson Leomiti, Darryl Moore, Tony Smith, Lawyer Tillman and Eric Weir.

A short time later, Dom Capers was named the team's first head coach. Capers had built a reputation as the defensive master mind of the Pittsburgh Steelers. In his three seasons as the defensive coordinator at Pittsburgh, the Steelers led the NFL in fewest points allowed.

Two weeks later, the Panthers selected 35 players in the expansion draft. Their first player selected was cornerback Rod Smith from the New England Patriots. Carolina quickly added two unrestricted free agents, kicker John Kasay from the Seahawks and defensive end Mike Fox from the New York Giants.

In the 1995 college draft, the Panthers used the fifth overall pick to grab Penn State University quarterback Kerry Collins.

The team's first training camp began July 14, 1995, at Wofford College in Spartanburg, S.C. The Panthers made their preseason debut against another expansion team, the Jacksonville Jaguars, at the Hall of Fame Game. The Panthers won, 20–14.

Carolina was impressive throughout the preseason, winning three of five games. The Panthers were equally impressive in their opening game, despite losing to the Atlanta Falcons, 23–20, in overtime. The Panthers continued to lose. They lost to the Buffalo Bills, 31–9, the St. Louis Rams, 31–10, the Tampa Bay Buccaneers, 20–13 and the Chicago Bears, 31–27. Then Carolina won its first game, a 26–15 win over the New York Jets, highlighted by Sam Mill's 36-yard interception return for a touchdown.

The Panthers then beat the New Orleans Saints, 20–3, New England, 20–17 in overtime, and the San Francisco 49ers, 13–7, for their fourth consecutive win, an NFL expansion team record. The win over the 49ers also marked the first time in league history that an expansion team beat the defending champion.

The Panthers wound up with a 7–9 record, more than doubling the previous best for wins by an NFL expansion team (3).

The following spring the Panthers selected running back Tshimanga Biakabutuka from the University of Michigan with the team's first-round pick in the college draft. The new Ericsson Stadium was initiated that fall. Optimism ran high among the Carolina faithful. However, reality told the faithful that the Panthers still were a second-year club.

Reality took a holiday in the 1996 NFL season. The Panthers won their season-opener over Atlanta, 29–6. They won Games 2 and 3, also. After losses to Jacksonville and Minnesota, the Panthers beat St. Louis and New Orleans. Carolina lost to the Philadelphia Eagles and Falcons, but closed out the regular season with seven consecutive wins over the Giants, Rams, Houston Oilers, Buccaneers, 49ers, Baltimore Ravens and Steelers. A 12–4 record, good enough for first place in the National Football Conference's Western Division. And a spot in the playoffs, too.

The Panthers bettered the defending Super Bowl champion Dallas Cowboys, 26–17, in the divisional playoffs. Carolina played error-free football. Collins threw two touchdown passes and running back Anthony Johnson gained 104 yards. Kasay booted four field goals.

The following week at Green Bay, the Panthers jumped in front of the Packers, 7–0, on a three-yard scoring pass from Collins to Howard Griffith. However, the eventual Super Bowl champ Packers wore down the Panthers and won, 30–13.

Capers was the consensus choice for coach of the year honors. He credited the players: "I've never been around a team where every player accepted his role like this one. The team had a special spirit that is something you try to capture every season."

McCormack retired from football following the season after 46 years in the business. He was replaced by Jon Richardson. The Panthers selected wide receiver Rae Carruth from the University of Colorado with their No. 1 pick in the college draft.

Carolina opened the 1997 season with a 24–10 loss against the Washington Redskins, then won back-to-back road games in Atlanta and San Diego. Three straight losses preceded three consecutive wins. The Panthers stood 5–4. However, Carolina, which had finished so strongly in each of its first two seasons, lost five of its final seven games. The Panthers were 7–9 and missed post-season play by two games.

Collins led the offense with 2,124 yards passing. He had 11 TDs, but threw 21 interceptions. Fred Lane led the team in rushing with 809 yards. Cornerback Eric Davis had five interceptions and linebacker Micheal Barrow had 8.5 sacks to lead the defense.

Carolina had given up just 218 points in 1996; it surrendered 314 points in '97.

*Kerry Collins was a Pro Bowler following the 1996 season.*

## INDIVIDUAL RECORDS

### Career

Rushing Yards: 1,588, Anthony Johnson, 1995–97

Passing Yards: 7,295, Kerry Collins, 1995–97

Receptions: 157, Mark Carrier, 1995–97

Interceptions: 10, Eric Davis, 1996–97

Touchdowns: 16, Wesley Walls, 1996–97

Points: 341, John Kasay, 1995–97

### Season

Rushing Yards: 1,120, Anthony Johnson, 1996

Passing Yards: 2,717, Kerry Collins, 1995

Receptions: 66, Mark Carrier, 1995

Interceptions: 6, Brett Maxie, 1995

Touchdowns: 10, Wesley Walls, 1996

Points: 145, John Kasay, 1996

## ACROSS

3. Position of the ball
6. Even
10. Carolina's region of the country
11. Path
12. Toss
14. A division
16. Lineman
17. Hole in the side of a helmet
18. Wager
20. After all or super
21. Rolled to a stop
23. Anthony and Chad
26. LB Bailey to friends
28. ___ and 10

29. Roaming DB
30. Real turf
32. Panthers' career rushing leader
34. Arm joint
38. Greg Kragen's position (init.)
39. Had team-record 6 interceptions in '95
40. Trods
41. Punt yards minus return yards
43. Rest on the bench
44. Go ___ it!
46. Elbow, shoulder or hip
47. Type of x-ray (init.)
49. 4th down boot
50. Hole

51. Crowd sound
56. Team meal: training ___
57. Ref's equipment
59. Squads
61. Unsigned player (init.)
63. On the back of a jersey (abbr.)
64. Foes
65. Team transportation from hotel to stadium

## DOWN

1. 1-on-1 (abbr.)
2. Jeff Zgonina's alma mater (init.)
3. Not enough
4. Points ___ turnovers
5. Panthers' head coach
6. Fans' beverage
7. Beaten
8. Missed FG: ___ good
9. Former
11. 51st Super Bowl?
13. Kevin Greene's position (abbr.)
15. Qtr.
16. Grabs hold
18. Led Panthers with 8.5 sacks in '97
19. 1st college player drafted by the Panthers

22. Home of the Redskins (init.)
23. College class of early entry draftees (abbr.)
24. Place for nasal strips
25. Player who begins the game
27. The ball is full of it
29. 3-pointer (init.)
30. WR Willie ___ had 46 catches in '96
31. Pass route: ___-in
33. Rental car company
35. Down and ___
36. Panthers' career scoring leader
37. Aide
42. Ref's relative
45. Blake Brockermeyer's position (init.)
48. Down and ___
49. Extra point (init.)
52. Faces
53. Double
54. Leg joint
55. Star of the game
58. Deflect
59. Knot
60. West coast foe (init.)
62. Stomach muscle (abbr.)

*Solution on page 184*

## RETIRED UNIFORM NUMBERS
None

```
S  B  A  R  R  O  W  S  S  E  T  A  B  G  N
A  K  U  T  U  B  A  K  A  I  B  A  R  T  I
N  T  O  T  K  C  L  I  A  M  S  I  E  M  E
C  A  P  E  R  S  G  R  L  C  F  N  T  A  L
E  L  S  M  H  R  S  S  O  F  P  I  L  X  R
X  E  D  S  E  H  O  I  I  Y  M  E  A  I  E
S  R  G  E  X  A  W  T  V  L  A  Y  W  E  U
O  V  N  M  T  A  H  L  V  A  S  L  O  I  E
I  R  E  O  L  N  J  A  H  N  D  P  T  S  B
R  E  C  L  G  O  N  T  T  G  R  E  E  N  E
U  V  S  U  H  O  P  H  U  R  E  L  L  I  M
T  I  A  N  S  G  W  O  R  M  C  A  A  L  E
N  L  S  L  A  A  R  N  R  O  E  N  A  L  D
E  O  E  L  R  Y  A  S  A  K  C  K  L  O  N
N  C  A  R  R  I  E  R  C  S  K  R  U  C  A
```

| | | |
|---|---|---|
| BARROW | COTA | LANE |
| BATES | DAVIS | LATHON |
| BEUERLEIN | GREEN | MAXIE |
| BIAKABUTUKA | GREENE | MILLER |
| CAPERS | GRIFFITH | OLIVER |
| CARRIER | ISMAIL | ROYAL |
| CARRUTH | JOHNSON | WALLS |
| COLLINS | KASAY | WALTER |

# CHICAGO BEARS

**G**eorge Halas, Red Grange, Bronko Nagurski, Gale Sayers, Dick Butkus and Walter Payton. They are some of the men who give the Chicago Bears one of the most storied histories in the National Football League, and helped the Bears win nine NFL championships.

No man in the history of professional sports, though, can compare to Halas. He was part of the franchise's birth in 1920 and remained part of the organization until his death in 1983. However, if not for the hip injury Halas suffered while playing right field for the New York Yankees—he preceded Babe Ruth at the position—the NFL would not exist as we know it today.

Following his baseball career-ending injury, Halas—who played in 12 games for the Yankees and got two hits in 22 at-bats—went to work in Decatur, Ill., for a corn products firm owned by A. E. Staley. The company already sponsored a semi-pro baseball team, and Staley wanted Halas to organize an independent football team. On Sept. 17, 1920, Halas, representing the Decatur Staleys, met with representatives of 12 other clubs at Ralph Hay's Hupmobile showroom in Canton, Ohio, and helped form the American Professional Football Association (which later became the NFL). The team membership fee was $100.

In that first season of 1920, the Decatur Staleys, with Halas as a co-coach, finished 10–1–2. They had 10 shutouts and lost only to the Chicago Cardinals, 7–6. Each player was paid $1,900 for the 13-week season. In 1921, Staley gave Halas the team and $5,000 to keep the name "Staleys" for one year. The team moved to Chicago and, playing in Wrigley Field, went 9–1–1 as it won its first championship. In 1922 the nickname was changed to "Bears." Chicago finished second (out of nearly 20 teams) in 1922, '23 and '24. At the conclusion of the 1924 season, Halas signed University of Illinois all-America halfback Harold "Red" Grange to the unbelievable sum of $100,000, although "The Galloping Ghost" couldn't play for the Bears until his collegiate career was over in a year.

The Bears went 9–5–3 in 1925. Following the season, Halas took Grange and the Bears on a 16-game coast-to-coast exhibition tour. The tour was a huge success, with more than 75,000 fans attending one game in Los Angeles.

Halas named Ralph Jones to replace himself as coach following the 1929 season. A year later, the Bears played in the first indoor football game in history. Playing on an 80-yard field at Chicago Stadium, the Bears and Cardinals played an exhibition game to raise money for unemployment relief.

The Bears returned to the Stadium in 1932 for a playoff game against the Portsmouth Spartans to break a regular-season tie. Nagurski hit Grange with a two-yard touchdown pass as the Bears won, 9–0. Halas returned as coach the following season, and the Bears won the first official championship game over the New York Giants, 23–21. The Bears became the first team to go undefeated and untied in the regular season in 1934, but lost to the Giants in the championship game, 30–13. Chicago was back in the title game in 1937 and lost to Washington, 28–21.

The Bears returned to the finals in 1940, at the beginning of pro football's modern era with the formal unveiling of the T-formation. They faced Washington in the championship game and scored 10 touchdowns on their way to a 70–0 blowout. The Bears won again in 1941, '43 and '46.

The Bears had to wait until 1963 to win it all again. That year, they intercepted five passes by Y. A. Tittle and beat the Giants, 14–10. In 1964 they slipped to 5–9, but found quick help in the 1965 college draft. With the third overall pick (which they had acquired in a trade with the Pittsburgh Steelers), they took Butkus, a linebacker out of the University of Illinois, and with the fourth overall selection (their own), they chose Sayers, a running back from the University of Kansas. The pair went on to become two of the greatest players in league history. Butkus was a seven-time all-pro; Sayers scored a record (since broken) 22 touchdowns in his rookie season and became the youngest player (34 years old) ever selected to the Pro Football Hall of Fame.

Halas retired as coach following the 1967 season with a record of 331–152–31 in 40 seasons. The Bears didn't make it back to postseason play until 1977, losing a playoff game to the Dallas Cowboys. The Bears also lost a Wild Card game to the Philadelphia Eagles in 1979. In 1982 fiery Mike Ditka, who played for Halas, was named the head coach. Two years later, Ditka led the Bears to the National Football Conference championship game before losing to the San Francisco 49ers. The following year, the Bears were in their first Super Bowl.

The game was a crowning achievement for Payton, the NFL's all-time leading rusher and one of the game's most popular players, who had suffered through several losing seasons. Although Payton did not stand out in the Super Bowl in New Orleans (61 yards rushing), the Bears hammered the New England Patriots, 46–10, as quarterback Jim McMahon passed for 256 yards. That team, which lost only one game all season, was one of the most successful and colorful in league history, with players such as William "Refrigerator" Perry, Steve McMichael, Richard Dent, Dan Hampton, Mike Singletary and Dave Duerson.

The Bears were in the playoffs five of the next six years, but never got back to the Super Bowl. They fell to 5–11 in 1992, and Ditka's popular and controversial reign came to an end. He was 112–68 in 11 seasons. Dave Wannstedt, a former assistant coach at Dallas, took over as head coach for the 1993 season.

The Bears improved to 7–9, then made the playoffs in 1994 with a 9–7 mark. However, the Bears failed to make post-season play in 1995 with a 9–7 record and slipped to 7–9 in '96 and 4–12 in '97.

*Erik Kramer threw for 3,000 yards in two seasons.*

## INDIVIDUAL RECORDS
### Career
Rushing Yards: 16,726, Walter Payton, 1975–87

Passing Yards: 14,686, Sid Luckman, 1939–50

Receptions: 492, Walter Payton, 1975–87

Interceptions: 38, Gary Fencik, 1976–87

Touchdowns: 125, Walter Payton, 1975–87

Points: 1,116, Kevin Butler, 1985–95

### Season
Rushing Yards: 1,852, Walter Payton, 1977

Passing Yards: 3,838, Erik Kramer, 1995

Receptions: 93, Johnny Morris, 1964

Interceptions: 10, Mark Carrier, 1990

Touchdowns: 22, Gale Sayers, 1965

Points: 144, Kevin Butler, 1985

## ACROSS

1. Bears' kicker, 1975–84
5. Guards
8. Try
10. Stadium signage
11. One-7th of a week
12. ___ Super Bowl
14. George Halas's alma mater (init.)
15. Dine
17. Try a 3-pointer (init.)
19. Against the rules
21. No. 51
23. TV talk: Hi, ___!
24. Wire service (init.)
25. Clock operator
27. Back-up player
29. Off-season activity
30. Type of x-ray (init.)
32. Not fast
35. Team leader
37. NFL's career rushing leader
39. Turn quickly
41. Squad
44. Pro bowler
46. Bears' career interceptions leader
47. FGA: It's ___, it's good!
48. Singletary or Ditka
49. Roll to a stop

50. 1st year players
54. Team transportation from hotel to stadium
55. A division
57. McMichael or Schubert
59. Blocks
60. Column heading on roster

## DOWN

1. Blocking scheme
2. Before sides or after Johns
3. Tied NFL record with 6 TDs in '65 game
4. Number representing action on the field
5. Carl Simpson's position (init.)
6. On the back of a jersey (abbr.)
7. RB Rashaan ___
9. Food at the training table
11. Bears' coach of Super Bowl team
13. Bears' all-time winningest coach
16. 3-pointer (init.)
17. Drop the ball
18. Bears' career passing leader

20. Keep your ___ on the ball
22. Forerunner to UPI (init.)
26. Used to clean up a shower
28. ___ vs. Them
31. ___ and 10
33. Practice before the game
34. Caught team-record 93 passes in '64
36. High in stature
38. Skein
39. DB
40. A lineman
42. Points ___ turnovers
43. Type of kickoff
45. Practice pants
47. Utilize
48. Face ___
51. One time
52. Position of the ball
53. DE John Thierry's alma mater (init.)
54. Wager
56. Try (abbr.)
58. Middle defensive lineman (init.)

*Solution on page 184*

## RETIRED UNIFORM NUMBERS

Bronko Nagurski—3
George McAfee—5
George Halas—7
Willie Galimore—28
Walter Payton—34
Gale Sayers—40
Brian Piccolo—41

Sid Luckman—42
Dick Butkus—51
Bill Hewitt—56
Bill George—61
Bulldog Turner—66
Red Grange—77

```
R  R  E  R  E  L  T  U  B  D  I  T  K  A  B
A  E  D  E  N  T  D  N  O  N  O  T  Y  A  P
T  A  M  X  C  Y  R  A  T  E  L  G  N  I  S
K  N  E  N  O  F  F  U  B  X  U  E  R  A  G
I  O  L  A  A  C  X  K  A  C  C  E  A  E  L
N  H  E  T  N  H  S  P  N  F  K  R  Y  N  E
S  A  A  R  O  S  I  R  R  O  M  E  I  R  U
E  M  H  B  S  R  D  N  B  L  A  M  Z  O  O
S  C  C  Z  R  H  C  O  U  U  N  A  A  H  G
T  M  I  R  E  I  R  R  A  C  T  R  L  N  R
S  R  M  J  D  M  L  U  J  A  C  K  L  A  A
A  A  C  U  N  D  U  N  F  K  T  H  U  V  N
L  I  M  H  A  O  B  S  A  M  O  H  T  S  G
A  S  A  Y  E  R  S  E  R  G  E  O  R  G  E
H  K  I  C  N  E  F  X  V  O  M  K  U  C  H
```

| | | |
|---|---|---|
| ANDERSON | DITKA | MCMAHON |
| ATKINS | FENCIK | MCMICHAEL |
| BUFFONE | GEORGE | MORRIS |
| BUTKUS | GRANGE | PAYTON |
| BUTLER | HALAS | SAYERS |
| CARRIER | KRAMER | SINGLETARY |
| COX | LUCKMAN | THOMAS |
| DENT | LUJACK | VAN HORNE |

# CINCINNATI BENGALS

**W**hen Paul Brown stepped down in 1962 as coach of the Cleveland Browns, he had won three National Football League championships, seven conference titles and 115 games in 13 seasons. A short time later, he had the urge to start a professional football team, but he had no idea his path would lead back to Ohio.

A study showed Cincinnati as a possible site for an expansion franchise. Brown was interested. In 1965 he met with Ohio's governor, and the pair agreed the state could support two pro football teams. In 1967 Brown's group of investors was awarded a franchise in the American Football League, and Brown was the first head coach.

Prior to their inaugural season of 1968, the Bengals acquired 40 veteran players in the expansion draft. They used their No. 1 pick in the college draft on University of Tennessee center Bob Johnson and also chose Bob Trumpy, Essex Johnson, Jess Phillips and Al Beauchamp. The Bengals went 3–11 that year. Paul Robinson, a third-round draft pick out of the University of Arizona, led the AFL in rushing with 1,023 yards and was named the Rookie of the Year.

The Bengals selected hometown quarterback Greg Cook and linebacker Bill Bergey in the draft the following year. They started the season 3–0, but finished with a 4–9–1 record. Brown was named the AFL Coach of the Year, Bergey was the AFL Defensive Rookie of the Year and Cook led the AFL in passing.

Cook threw out his arm in training camp prior to the 1970 season, however, and Virgil Carter was signed to play quarterback. Cincinnati lost six of its first seven games, but won its final seven games for an 8–6 mark. The Bengals won the AFC Central Division title and were in the playoffs in just their third season, the earliest any expansion team qualified for postseason play. The Bengals lost to the Baltimore Colts, 17–0, but that didn't dampen the excitement generated throughout southern Ohio.

The Bengals added quarterback Ken Anderson the following year and rolled to a 5–0–1 preseason record. They won their opener, then lost seven straight games, and finished 4–10. They righted themselves in 1972, going 8–6, then got back in the playoffs in 1973 with a 10–4 record and another division title. They lost to the Miami Dolphins, 34–16, in the divisional playoffs.

Anderson won the NFL passing title in 1974, but the Bengals were just 7–7. The next year was Brown's last as a head coach and turned out to be the Bengals' best, record-wise. They started the season with six straight wins and wound up 11–3, and Anderson won his second straight passing title. Still, the Bengals again were eliminated in the first round of the playoffs.

Bill Johnson was named Brown's replacement for the 1976 season. The Bengals won nine of their first 11 games, but fell to 10–4 and out of postseason play. Cornerback Ken Riley led the American Football Conference with nine interceptions.

The Bengals remained competitive in 1977, going 8–6, but then lost their first five games in 1978. Johnson was fired, and Homer Rice took over. The Bengals slid to 1–12 before winning their final three games of the season.

Cincinnati had its second straight 4–12 record in 1979 and improved slightly to 6–10 in 1980. Prior to the 1980 season the Bengals named Forrest Gregg the head coach and used their No. 1 draft pick to acquire Anthony Munoz. The offensive tackle from the University of Southern California was a 12-time Pro Bowl pick in his 13 seasons in Cincinnati.

The Bengals unveiled new uniforms, including tiger-striped helmets, in 1981, and the team's performance seemed to reflect their new look as they went 12–4 and won the Central Division. They beat the Buffalo Bills, 28–21, in the divisional playoff, and the San Diego Chargers, 27–7, in the AFC title game, to earn a trip to the Super Bowl. Facing the San Francisco 49ers in Pontiac, Mich., the Bengals rolled up 356 yards, compared to 275 for the 49ers, but lost, 26–21.

The Bengals were 7–2 in the strike-shortened 1982 season, but lost in the first round of the playoffs. After a 7–9 mark in 1983, Gregg was succeeded by Sam Wyche. The Bengals went 8–8, then 7–9 under Wyche, but quarterback Boomer Esiason was developing into one of the league's best.

The Bengals improved to 10–6 in 1986, then slumped to 4–11 the following season. In 1988, however, they executed the biggest one-year turnaround in NFL history by going 12–4, and Esiason was named the league's MVP. The Bengals beat the Seattle Seahawks and Buffalo to advance to the Super Bowl and again faced the 49ers. They took a 16–13 lead on Jim Breech's 40-yard field goal with 3:20 remaining in the game, but Joe Montana led the 49ers on a 92-yard, 11-play drive that resulted in a touchdown with 34 seconds left. The Bengals lost, 20–16.

The Bengals fell to 8–8 in 1989, but were 9–7 and back in the playoffs in 1990. They beat the Houston Oilers, then lost to the Los Angeles Raiders. They tumbled all the way to 3–13 in 1991, and Wyche was replaced by Dave Shula, son of Miami Dolphin's coach Don Shula.

The Bengals won only 19 of 71 games under Shula. He was replaced after seven games into the 1996 season by Bruce Coslet. The Bengals rallied under Coslet, winning seven of their last nine games to finish 8–8. In 1997, after a 1–7 start, the Bengals again finished strong, winning six of their final eight games.

The Bengals offense has been led by quarterback Jeff Blake who is a true double threat. In the last two seasons, he has passed for 5,453 yards and rushed for 551. He has accounted for 37 touchdowns (32 by passing). The Bengals' 1997 second-round draft choice, Cory Dillon from the University of Washington, led the team with 1,129 yards rushing.

*Copyright © 1997 Michael C. Hebert/Spurlock Photography, Inc.*

*Jeff Blake has thrown 74 touchdown passes and only 48 interceptions.*

## INDIVIDUAL RECORDS

### Career

Rushing Yards:  6,447, James Brooks, 1984–91

Passing Yards:  32,838, Ken Anderson, 1971–86

Receptions:  417, Cris Collinsworth, 1981–88

Interceptions:  65, Ken Riley, 1969–83

Touchdowns:  70, Pete Johnson, 1977–83

Points:  1,151, Jim Breech, 1980–92

### Season

Rushing Yards:  1,239, James Brooks, 1989

Passing Yards:  3,959, Boomer Esiason, 1986

Receptions:  100, Carl Pickens, 1996

Interceptions:  9, Ken Riley, 1976

Touchdowns:  17, Carl Pickens, 1995

Points:  121, Doug Pelfrey, 1995

## ACROSS

3. TD + safety
8. Scored team-record 70 TDs from 1977–83
10. Column heading on roster
12. Small amount of light
13. Type of x-ray (init.)
14. Stadium signage
16. Night before a game
17. Squad
19. Bengals' career rushing leader
23. Tony McGee's position (init.)
24. ___ or die
25. Post-game media session
28. Bengals' head coach
29. Passing formation
31. Turn sharply
32. Usual college game day (abbr.)
34. Down and ___
35. Coaching family members
37. On two. Ready, ___!
39. Former
40. Other Sunday bench
41. Supervised trip
43. 2nd Super Bowl
45. John Copeland's position (init.)
46. Set a team record with 121 points in '95
49. Isaac
50. Publicity (init.)

53. Between players

55. Bengals' career scoring leader

56. Boomer

59. Free weekend

60. Block

61. Crowd sounds

63. East Carolina QB

64. Regulations

## DOWN

1. Bills' Simpson

2. Bengals' career passing leader

3. A lineman

4. Contest

5. Shown on the scoreboard

6. Easy FG: ___ shot

7. Eye

9. 22-years-___

11. Stop play

14. 200 Cinergy Field and 280 Park Ave.

15. Bengals' career receiving leader

18. Away

20. Rests on the bench

21. All-pro turned coach

22. Scored team-record 4 TDs in '84 game

26. Point value of a safety

27. Bengals' coach, 1984–91

30. Assist

33. 6-pointer (abbr.)

36. Trod

38. Important read

40. Caught team-record 100 passes in '96

42. FGA: It's ___, it's good!

44. Bengals' career interceptions leader

47. Had team-record 3 interceptions in '89 game

48. Quarter

51. TV talk: ___, Mom!

52. Office betting games

54. Championship

57. Vend

58. Stomach muscle (abbr.)

62. Where severely injured players are sent (init.)

*Solution on page 185*

---

**RETIRED UNIFORM NUMBER**

Bob Johnson—54

```
E  H  S  I  R  R  A  P  J  B  L  A  K  E  E
K  N  G  N  O  T  T  U  O  Z  U  E  D  S  P
I  B  R  O  W  N  P  G  H  H  I  U  I  C  E
N  Y  R  E  T  R  A  C  N  B  S  A  L  O  L
N  S  I  M  I  I  G  D  S  N  S  W  L  L  F
E  I  L  C  A  E  I  R  O  O  A  I  O  L  R
B  T  E  D  R  X  T  A  N  A  M  L  N  I  E
R  X  Y  T  O  E  R  T  R  E  B  K  U  N  Y
E  S  T  N  R  H  V  O  O  D  R  I  T  S  C
W  N  I  T  R  A  M  T  L  C  O  N  A  W  U
D  E  C  O  S  L  E  T  S  R  S  S  U  O  R
Y  K  X  N  E  A  L  C  A  I  E  O  O  R  T
K  C  R  S  K  O  O  R  B  U  W  N  E  T  I
J  I  N  H  B  R  E  E  C  H  R  E  S  H  S
B  P  A  N  D  E  R  S  O  N  E  L  L  Y  M
```

| | | |
|---|---|---|
| AMBROSE | COSLET | MARTIN |
| ANDERSON | CURTIS | PARRISH |
| BLAKE | DILLON | PELFREY |
| BREECH | DIXON | PICKENS |
| BROOKS | ESIASON | PRICE |
| BROWN | JOHNSON | RILEY |
| CARTER | KINNEBREW | SCOTT |
| COLLINSWORTH | LEWIS | WILKINSON |

# DALLAS COWBOYS

**A**merica's team. As the featured squad in the second game of a televised doubleheader on CBS nearly every Sunday each fall, the Dallas Cowboys became a fixture in most of the country's homes for 20 years. The lineup was the same everywhere: the local National Football Conference team, the Cowboys and *60 Minutes*. However, the Cowboys often were liked better than the locals and better known than Mike Wallace.

The names and numbers—always, it seemed, on white jerseys—became known to even the casual fan for two generations. No. 12, Roger Staubach. No. 74, "Mr. Cowboy" Bob Lilly. No. 17, "Dandy Don" Meredith. No. 43, Don Perkins. No. 54, Chuck Howley. No. 20, Mel Renfro. No. 55, Lee Roy Jordan. No. 33, Tony Dorsett. And more recently, No. 8, Troy Aikman. No. 22, Emmitt Smith. And No. 88, Michael Irvin.

Television viewers watched the Cowboys because they were winners. They have won five Super Bowls and played in three others. They watched them because they were exciting. And some watched them because of the cheerleaders, in white boots and bare midriffs.

However, no one could have predicted the Cowboys' immense popularity when Dallas was granted a National Football League franchise in 1960. The Cowboys lost their opening game to the Pittsburgh Steelers, 35–28, and went 0–11–1 that first season. Eddie LeBaron was the first quarterback, and the leading rusher was L. G. Dupre. Head coach Tom Landry and general manager Tex Schramm weren't too concerned.

The Cowboys won three of their first four games the following season and wound up an encouraging 4–9–1. They continued to improve, and in 1965 went 7–7 in the regular season, good for a second-place tie in the Eastern Conference. By then Meredith was the starting quarterback and Perkins was the leading ground gainer. A year later, the Cowboys were in their first championship game. They won their conference with a 10–3–1 record and faced the Green Bay Packers for the right to represent the NFL in the first Super Bowl. The Packers won, 34–27. The two teams had a rematch in the NFC championship game the next year, but Green Bay won again in the famous "Ice Bowl" in sub-zero weather, 21–17. Still, the Cowboys had arrived.

Dallas won six straight conference or division titles starting in 1966. Prior to the 1969 season Meredith, the last of the original Cowboys, announced his retirement, but that was also the year the Cowboys finally got to bring in their 10th-round pick from the 1964 draft, Staubach, who had been serving in the Navy.

The Cowboys made it to the Super Bowl for the first time in 1970, but lost to the Baltimore Colts when rookie kicker Jim O'Brien booted a 32-yard field goal with five seconds remaining to give the Colts a 16–13 win.

The Cowboys were back in the Super Bowl the following year and beat the Miami Dolphins, 24–3. In 1972, Calvin Hill became the first Cowboy to rush for 1,000 yards, and Dallas qualified for the playoffs a record seventh straight season. The Cowboys made it eight in a row in 1973, but fell to the Minnesota Vikings, 27–10, in the NFC championship game.

The Cowboys were out of postseason play in 1974, but returned to the Super Bowl in '75. They lost to Pittsburgh, 21–17.

Dallas continued to dominate the NFC throughout the rest of the 1970s, as it again won or tied for the division title six straight years. The Cowboys won the Super Bowl in 1977 (27–10 over the Denver Broncos) and lost to Pittsburgh in 1978 (35–31 in Super Bowl XIII).

Dorsett arrived in 1977 and ran for more than 12,000 yards over a 10-year career. Staubach retired in 1979 and was replaced at quarterback by Danny White. The Cowboys continued their winning ways until 1986 when they went 7–9 and snapped a streak of 20 consecutive winning seasons. That represented the third longest streak in professional sports history, surpassed only by the New York Yankees (39 straight winning seasons, 1926–64) and the Montreal Canadiens (32 from 1952–83).

After a third straight losing season in 1988, owner Bum Bright sold the team to Jerry Jones. The new owner immediately fired Landry (with a lifetime record of 270–178–6), enraging local fans, and named Jimmy Johnson the head coach. Two months later Schramm resigned. The only consolation for the fans was the Cowboys had the No. 1 pick in the draft and selected Aikman.

The Cowboys plummeted to 1–15 in the first season under the new regime. This time they used their first-round draft choice to select Smith, and their fortunes began to turn around. They improved to 7–9, and Johnson was named the NFL Coach of the Year. Then in 1991, with Smith leading the league in rushing yards and Irvin leading in receiving yards, the Cowboys went 11–5 and were back in the playoffs.

Dallas continued its improvement into 1992, finishing 13–3. The Cowboys beat the Philadelphia Eagles and San Francisco 49ers to advance to the Super Bowl where they crushed the Buffalo Bills, 52–17. The following year the Cowboys (12–4) were back in the Super Bowl for a league-record seventh time and won a rematch over Buffalo, 30–13. However, despite the back-to-back titles, all was not well. Johnson wore out his welcome, and Jones replaced him with former University of Oklahoma coach Barry Switzer two months after the celebrating ended.

The Cowboys didn't miss a beat with the new coach. They won three more divisional titles and defeated Pittsburgh, 27–17, to win Super Bowl XXX following the 1995 season.

Off the field turmoil wreaked havoc on the Cowboys on the field in the 1997 season and Dallas stumbled to a 6–10 record. Jones wasted little time in replacing Switzer with Chan Gailey, the offensive coordinator for the Steelers.

*Copyright © 1995 Michael C. Hebert/Spurlock Photography, Inc.*

*Deion Sanders is the only man to play in the Super Bowl and the World Series.*

## INDIVIDUAL RECORDS

### Career

Rushing Yards: 12,036, Tony Dorsett, 1977–87

Passing Yards: 26,016, Troy Aikman, 1989–97

Receptions: 666, Michael Irvin, 1988–97

Interceptions: 52, Mel Renfro, 1964–77

Touchdowns: 119, Emmitt Smith, 1990–97

Points: 874, Rafael Septien, 1978–86

### Season

Rushing Yards: 1,773, Emmitt Smith, 1995

Passing Yards: 3,980, Danny White, 1983

Receptions: 111, Michael Irvin, 1995

Interceptions: 11, Everson Walls, 1981

Touchdowns: 25, Emmitt Smith, 1995

Points: 150, Emmitt Smith, 1995

## ACROSS

4. Drew or Preston
7. Ball prop
8. Out of bounds marking
10. TV talk: ___, Mom!
11. Had team-record 13 catches in '67 game
12. Extra point (init.)
14. Cowboys' career receiving leader
16. Deflect a FGA (init.)
19. Treatment for a sprained ankle
20. Pull the ball away
23. QB recorded C&W song "Oklahoma Nights"
25. Contest
27. Roger the Dodger
29. Cowboys' career rushing leader
31. Hurvin McCormack's alma mater (init.)
33. Meaty team meal
36. Before side or after Johns
37. Up and ___
38. 2 safeties
40. Olympic sprinter turned WR
41. Rested on the bench
43. Aikman's computer step: log-___
46. On the back of a jersey (abbr.)
47. Enthusiasm

49. Emporia State DT
50. Had team-record 3 interceptions in '71 game
54. Former mode of team travel
56. Paid player
57. Triceps exercise
58. Led the Cowboys in sacks 7 times from 1974–82
61. Rushes
62. Had team-record 5 sacks in '66 game
66. Logo registration (abbr.)
67. Jay Novacek's position (init.)
68. Slate of games

## DOWN

1. Help on a tackle
2. Stadium signage
3. 2nd Super Bowl
4. RB wore No. 43 from 1961–68
5. Golfer Palmer
6. Large, medium and small
7. Deflect
9. Kicker ___ Elliott
13. Stop in play
15. 3rd Super Bowl
17. Scuffle
18. Emmitt, Kevin or Vinson
21. We'll tell you later (init.)
22. ___-announcer (init.)
24. 4th down boot
26. Butch, Mike or Undra
28. 6-pointer (abbr.)
30. Cowboys' coach, 1994–97
32. Crowd sound of displeasure
33. Usual college class of draftee (abbr.)
34. Danny, Randy or Bob
35. Dandy Don
39. Before defeated or sportsmanlike
42. Unsigned player (init.)
44. Alabama LB wore No. 55 from 1963–76
45. Try (abbr.)
48. Cowboys' 1st coach
51. Billy Joe
52. Column heading on roster
53. Recreational activity
54. Go ___ guy
55. Stomach muscle (abbr.)
59. Type of tackle
60. Leg joint
63. Fred Strickland's position (abbr.)
64. 1st word of the national anthem
65. Team doctor (init.)

*Solution on page 185*

---

## RETIRED UNIFORM NUMBERS

None

```
O   R   F   N   E   R   N   S   A   N   D   E   R   S   N
N   N   N   A   K   E   C   A   V   O   N   H   W   O   H
P   T   O   I   E   N   V   O   K   I   A   T   O   R   T
S   E   I   R   T   T   L   I   L   L   Y   I   O   L   I
T   Q   R   W   R   Z   I   B   A   K   H   M   D   Z   D
S   U   M   K   N   E   W   T   O   N   C   S   S   C   E
E   E   N   S   I   L   X   S   L   L   A   W   O   Z   R
N   S   A   I   E   N   W   M   Y   R   B   P   N   Y   E
O   T   D   N   L   Y   S   I   E   D   U   H   O   E   M
J   T   R   I   O   A   A   P   L   U   A   E   K   L   R
T   E   O   V   A   J   N   H   W   B   T   H   G   R   E
S   S   J   R   U   L   D   O   I   S   R   E   E   P
U   R   A   I   K   M   A   N   H   I   E   E   R   D   M
O   O   Y   T   A   E   C   W   R   E   K   M   R   D   E
H   D   L   A   N   D   R   Y   N   R   S   E   E   A   K
```

| | | |
|---|---|---|
| ADDERLEY | JORDAN | RENFRO |
| AIKMAN | LANDRY | RENTZEL |
| DORSETT | LILLY | SANDERS |
| GREEN | MEREDITH | SMITH |
| HAYES | NEWTON | STAUBACH |
| HOWLEY | NILAND | WALLS |
| IRVIN | NOVACEK | WHITE |
| JONES | PERKINS | WOODSON |

# DENVER BRONCOS

In the first 13 years of their existence, the Denver Broncos never had a winning season.

Enter John Ralston. In five years, Ralston led the Broncos to a winning record three times, including a 9–5 mark in his final season of 1976. Even though he made Denver competitive, he still wasn't able to get the Broncos into the playoffs.

Enter Red Miller. In his first season as the head coach in 1977, he not only guided the Broncos to a league-best 12–2 record, he also got them into the playoffs for the first time. He then took it one step further, leading the Broncos into Super Bowl XII in 1978. In four years, Miller's teams were 40–22 with three playoff appearances.

Enter Dan Reeves. In 12 seasons as the head coach, Reeves led the Broncos to a 117–79–1 record. They were under .500 just once. Denver made the playoffs six times and advanced to the Super Bowl three times. However, the Broncos never returned to the Mile High City with the world championship.

Following two difficult years with Wade Phillips at the helm, enter Mike Shanahan. The former offensive coordinator of the San Francisco 49ers, Shanahan had experienced success in the Super Bowl. His goal wasn't just to get Denver into another title game; his goal was for Denver to win it.

The Broncos finished 8–8 in Shanahan's first year, 1995. They improved to a league-best 13–3 the following season, but were upset by the Jacksonville Jaguars, 30–27, in the divisional playoffs.

Denver returned for the 1997 season with a vengeance. The Broncos won their first six games en route to a 12–4 mark. They got revenge on Jacksonville in the first round of the playoffs, beating the Jaguars, 42–17. The Broncos edged the Kansas City Chiefs, 14–10, then the Pittsburgh Steelers, 24–21, to advance to Super Bowl XXXII in San Diego.

The Broncos stunned the heavily favored Green Bay Packers, 31–24, for the first Super Bowl title in Denver's history.

The wait was long, but worth it. Denver was just happy to be one of the original six cities represented at the first American Football League organizational meeting at Chicago in 1959. The principal owner was Bob Howsam. He selected players through 32 rounds of the draft, with Trinity College center Roger LeClerc. Two weeks later Howsam named a general manager, Dean Griffing, and a month after that, the Broncos had their first coach, Frank Filchock.

After losing all five of its preseason games, Denver became the first AFL winner when it beat the Patriots in Boston, 13–10, in the first scheduled game. The Broncos finished the season 4–9–1. End Lionel Taylor, tackle Bud McFadin and safety Goose Gonsoulin all were named to the first all-AFL team.

The Broncos struggled throughout their years in the AFL, finished last or next to last in their division nine out of 10 years. Their best finish was 7–7 in 1962, but that still left them four games out of the playoffs.

Among the Broncos of note in the AFL days were cornerback Willie Wood (1963–66), who was an all-league pick in 1964 when he intercepted nine passes, including a club-record four in one game, quarterback Frank Tripucka (1960–63), the father of former professional basketball player Kelly Tripucka, and holder of the team's single-game record for passing yards (447) and passing touchdowns (five), and running back Floyd Little (1967–75), who is the club's all-time rushing and touchdowns leader.

When the AFL merged with the National Football League for the 1970 season, the Broncos were part of the American Football Conference's Western Division with the Oakland Raiders, Kansas City Chiefs and San Diego Chargers. The Broncos continued to struggle until Ralston arrived in 1972. Denver improved to 7–5–2 in 1973, then hovered around .500 until 1976 when it was 9–5. Ralston departed and was replaced by Miller. Quarterback Craig Morton arrived at the same time in a trade with the New York Giants.

That pair led the Broncos to a 12–2 record in 1977 and the club's first division championship. Denver beat Pittsburgh, 34–21, in the first round of the playoffs, then won the AFC championship over Oakland, 20–17. That set the stage for the Broncos' first trip to the Super Bowl. They faced the Dallas Cowboys in what was at that time the most-watched sporting event in television history. The Cowboys jumped out to a 13–0 halftime lead and coasted to a 27–10 victory.

The Broncos were aiming higher the following season. They again won the AFC Western Division, but lost in the divisional playoffs to Pittsburgh, 33–10. The Broncos were 10–6 in 1979 and a Wild Card team in the playoffs, but lost in the first round to the Houston Oilers, 13–7. In 1980 they slipped to 8–8, out of the playoffs, and Miller was gone. Reeves kept them competitive until 1983 when the Broncos traded two first-round draft picks and Mark Herrmann to the Indianapolis Colts for the rights to rookie quarterback John Elway.

That trade marked a turning point. The Broncos made the playoffs with a 9–7 record in Elway's first season, and reached the Super Bowl in 1986. They lost to the Giants, however, 39–20. They returned to the Super Bowl the following season, but lost to the Washington Redskins, 42–10. After a .500 season in 1988, the Broncos reached the Super Bowl again in 1989, but lost to the San Francisco 49ers, 55–10.

Denver slid to 5–11 in 1990, but were back in the playoffs in '91, '93 and '96 before their Super Bowl victory following the '97 season.

The championship was especially important for Elway. Despite throwing for nearly 50,000 yards in his 15-year NFL career, he carried the unofficial tag of "best quarterback who never won a championship."

*John Elway led the Broncos to a victory in Super Bowl XXXII.*

## INDIVIDUAL RECORDS

### Career

Rushing Yards:  6,323, Floyd Little, 1967–75

Passing Yards:  48,669, John Elway, 1983–97

Receptions:  543, Lionel Taylor, 1960–66

Interceptions:  44, Steve Foley, 1976–86

Touchdowns:  54, Floyd Little, 1967–75

Points:  742, Jim Turner, 1971–79

### Season

Rushing Yards:  1,750, Terrell Davis, 1997

Passing Yards:  4,030, John Elway, 1993

Receptions:  100, Lionel Taylor, 1961

Interceptions:  11, Goose Gonsoulin, 1960

Touchdowns:  15, Terrell Davis, 1996 and 1997

Points:  137, Gene Mingo, 1962

## ACROSS

1. College class of early entry draftee
3. Fumble or interception
8. Broncos' leading receiver in '97
10. Neil Smith's position (init.)
11. Shove
14. Wide right
15. 3rd Super Bowl
16. Go ___ guy
17. Time zone for Redskins (init.)
18. NFL championship game
21. Outside of LG
22. Mistakes
24. Broncos' conference (init.)
25. 2 safeties
27. Call at coin flip
29. Broncos' career rushing leader
31. WR Zach Thomas' alma mater (init.)
32. ___-captain
33. Beyond RT
36. Richard Dickinson's nickname
37. Them
38. Threw for a team-record 447 yards in '62 game
41. Fewer
44. Championship
46. Broncos' career interceptions leader
47. Perspiration

48. Weird
50. HB
51. Begins the game
52. 9th Super Bowl
53. Down and ___
56. Qtr.
57. Ouch!
58. Mix
59. Ball prop
61. Plead
62. Whirlpool
63. Broncos' coach, 1981–92
65. Head protection
66. Tally

## DOWN

1. Top half of a uniform
2. Broncos' single-season rusher leader
3. Shannon Sharpe's position (init.)
4. Outside of RG
5. Do we punt ___ try a field goal?
6. List of players
7. Star of the game
8. Detron, Neil or Rod
9. Bills' LB Bryce ___
12. Injure
13. Gonsoulin
14. Broncos' stadium
16. Broncos' career scoring leader

19. Had more than 3,000 yards in punt returns from 1975–83
20. Has won more games as a starter than any QB in history
23. ___ or die
24. Path of a pass
25. Pick up a loose ball (init.)
26. ___ vs. Them
28. Informant
30. Broncos' career receiving leader
34. Simple
35. Tied NFL record with 4 interceptions in '64 game
37. Knotted
39. Participant
40. Selected to play in the McDonald's HS All-America basketball game
42. Arm joints
43. WR
45. Get beaten
49. Leaps
54. Swap
55. Bruce Plummer's alma mater (init.)
56. Stack of bodies
59. Part of foot kicking the ball
60. Yards punted minus punt return
61. Wager
64. No attempt to return a punt (init.)

*Solution on page 186*

---

**RETIRED UNIFORM NUMBERS**

Frank Tripucka—18

Floyd Little—44

```
D  N  O  S  T  A  W  L  A  S  T  C  T  S  H
T  D  I  I  S  I  V  A  D  H  A  R  H  U  C
C  B  R  Y  A  N  N  D  R  E  M  O  R  R
E  N  N  A  L  O  H  I  T  E  O  T  M  E  U
L  D  O  R  W  N  S  E  T  R  I  E  P  H  H
W  S  L  M  R  O  R  R  T  N  C  H  S  C  C
A  L  U  S  I  A  H  O  R  K  F  T  O  T  P
Y  A  O  T  G  L  N  D  L  E  O  I  N  E  U
Y  N  U  R  H  G  C  E  C  R  C  M  N  L  M
P  O  C  O  T  K  N  U  E  O  R  S  D  F  A
T  S  X  N  C  B  J  D  P  O  D  O  M  S  L
S  K  T  G  U  I  N  S  L  R  I  C  H  D  E
Y  C  N  R  A  I  D  Y  S  U  O  V  A  H  C
V  A  G  V  W  R  A  T  U  R  N  E  R  G  M
P  J  L  I  T  T  L  E  C  H  Y  E  L  O  F
```

| | | |
|---|---|---|
| ARMSTRONG | FOLEY | SMITH |
| BRYAN | HOWARD | TAYLOR |
| CARTER | JACKSON | THOMPSON |
| CHAVOUS | LANIER | TURNER |
| DAVIS | LITTLE | UPCHURCH |
| ELAM | MECKLENBURG | WATSON |
| ELWAY | MORTON | WINDER |
| FLETCHER | ODOMS | WRIGHT |

# DETROIT LIONS

The Lions wasted no time in making an impression on their home fans when they began play in Detroit in 1934. They won their first seven games, all by shutouts, by a combined score of 118–0. They won their next three games, too, to run their victory string to 10. That's still the longest single-season winning streak in club history.

It was the summer of 1934 when Detroit radio executive George Richards purchased the Portsmouth (Ohio) Spartans for less than $8,000 and moved the franchise to the Motor City. Portsmouth had gained a franchise in 1930 and had been competitive during its four-year history.

The Lions weren't the first professional football team in Detroit, however. In 1920 the Detroit Heralds were a charter member of the American Professional Football Association, which evolved into the National Football League. The Heralds folded after two years. In 1925 the Detroit Panthers were formed, but they lasted just two seasons. The Detroit Wolverines came to be in 1928, but lasted for only a year.

The Lions didn't win the championship in their inaugural season in 1934, but they won the title in 1935, beating the New York Giants, 26–7. That team was coached by George "Potsy" Clark and featured "Dutch" Clark, "Ace" Gutowsky and "Ox" Emerson.

Detroit didn't get back into the playoffs until 1952, but that year began a six-year run in which the Lions reached the championship game four times and won three titles. They won back-to-back championships in 1952 and '53. The coach was Buddy Parker and the stars were future Hall of Famers Bobby Layne, Jack Christiansen and Doak Walker.

The Lions lost to the Cleveland Browns in the 1954 championship game, but won again in '57 when they beat the Browns, 59–14, in the title match.

The Lions struggled throughout the 1960s, but in 1970 qualified for the playoffs with a 10–4 record. They lost in the divisional playoffs to the Dallas Cowboys, 5–0 (contrary to rumors, Denny McLain was not the losing pitcher).

The rest of the '70s were tragic for the Lions. Not only did they miss postseason competition, they suffered more important losses. During a game in 1971, wide receiver Chuck Hughes suffered a heart attack and died on the field. Then in the summer of 1974, just a year-and-a-half after being named the Lions' head coach, Don McCafferty died of a heart attack.

The best news of the decade came just prior to the 1975 season when the Lions moved into their new home, a domed stadium in Pontiac, Mich. The Silverdome, seating more than 80,000 fans, is the world's largest air-supported dome in the world.

Detroit's fortunes took a turn in 1980. The Lions selected University of Oklahoma running back Billy Sims with the No. 1 pick in the college draft. He had an immediate impact, as the Lions tied for the National Football Conference's Central Division title (but missed the playoffs because of tie-breakers). They were 8–8 in 1981, then made the playoffs in the strike-shortened season of 1982 despite their 4–5 record, because they finished in the top eight of the NFC. Detroit lost in the first round of the "Super Bowl Tournament" to the Washington Redskins, 31–7.

The Lions returned to the playoffs in 1983 after winning their division with a 9–7 mark. However, they missed a last-second field goal attempt and lost to the San Francisco 49ers in the first round, 24–23.

Following a 4–11–1 record in 1984, head coach Monte Clark and his entire coaching staff were fired. Darryl Rogers, of nearby Michigan State University, was named the new head coach. Rogers last just three-and-a-half seasons, and he was replaced by Wayne Fontes.

Under Fontes, the Lions struggled for two seasons before returning to prominence in 1991. With the emergence of running back Barry Sanders (the NFC's MVP), special teams player Mel Gray (who became the first player in NFL history to lead the league in both kickoff and punt return average in the same season), and defenders Bennie Blades, Chris Spielman and Jerry Ball, Detroit went 12–4 and won its division. The Lions recorded their first playoff win since 1957 with a 38–6 victory over Dallas, but lost in the NFC title game to Washington, 41–10.

Expectations were high entering the 1992 season. The Lions lost their season opener with the Chicago Bears, 27–24, but beat the Minnesota Vikings. Then Detroit lost by three points at Washington, by four points to the Tampa Bay Buccaneers and by six points against the New Orleans Saints. Before they knew what hit them, they were 1–4, and the losses had come by a total of 16 points. The Lions never recovered and wound up 5–11.

However, in 1993, the Lions were victorious in seven of their first nine games and won the division with a 10–6 record. They beat the Green Bay Packers in the season finale to earn home-field advantage in the playoffs, but lost, 28–24, the following week in a rematch with the Packers.

Detroit was back in the playoffs in 1994 and '95, but were beaten in the first round. The 1996 team slid to 5–11. The following season, led by Sanders' 2,053 yards rushing, the Lions went 9–7 and were back in postseason play.

*Copyright © 1997 Jay Cribfield/Spurlock Photography, Inc.*

*Barry Sanders has rushed for 13,778 yards, second on the NFL's all-time list.*

## INDIVIDUAL RECORDS

### Career

Rushing Yards:  13,778, Barry Sanders, 1989–97

Passing Yards:  15,710, Bobby Layne, 1950–58

Receptions:  528, Herman Moore, 1991–97

Interceptions:  62, Dick LeBeau, 1959–72

Touchdowns:  105, Barry Sanders, 1989–97

Points:  1,113, Eddie Murray, 1980–91

### Season

Rushing Yards:  2,053, Barry Sanders, 1997

Passing Yards:  4,338, Scott Mitchell, 1995

Receptions:  123, Herman Moore, 1995

Interceptions:  12, Don Doll, 1950, and Jack Christiansen, 1953

Touchdowns:  17, Barry Sanders, 1991

Points:  132, Jason Hanson, 1995

## ACROSS

2. Arm joints
5. ___-announcer (init.)
6. Lions' career scoring leader
10. Turn sharply
11. Fumbles and interceptions (abbr.)
12. DB Jimmy or DB Nate
13. West coast city without NFL team (init.)
14. Column heading on roster
15. '89 Heisman Trophy winner
18. Helps with a tackle
21. Fail to catch a pass
22. Reggie Brown's position (abbr.)

24. TV talk: ___, Mom!
25. Threw for team-record 410 yards in '95 game
27. East coast rival (init.)
28. Tally
30. Potsy
31. HB
33. ___ Parseghian
34. Publicity (init.)
35. Mel, Mike or Miller
36. Against (abbr.)
37. Twirlers' equipment
38. Down and ___
39. Sign a pact
41. 6-pointer (abbr.)

43. ___ the ball!

47. DE was Lions' No. 1 pick in '92

50. Delayed run

52. Go ___ it!

55. Had 56 interceptions from 1967–77

56. Steal

58. Lions' coach, 1988–96

59. Protection for broken bone

61. Usual game day (abbr.)

64. Pass ___ run?

65. ___ way or the highway!

66. Designate

## DOWN

1. Off-season underwater activity

2. Expected time for landing (init.)

3. Game spheres

4. Was victorious

5. Plot

6. Lions' career receiving leader

7. ___ vs. Them

8. Lions' coach, 1985–88

9. Column heading on roster (abbr.)

13. Lions' career passing leader and family

16. Toy player

17. A unit of players on fourth down

19. Lions' career tackles leader

20. Sunday night game cable network (init.)

23. One-third of a yard

25. Caught passes for more than 1,000 yards in '97

26. Runner with the ball

28. Pull the ball away

29. A division

32. Threw for team-record 5 TDs in '78 game

40. DT turned actor

42. ___ or die

44. On the back of jerseys

45. West coast foe (init.)

46. Blocking schemes

48. '70 Heisman Trophy winner from Oklahoma

49. ___-captain

51. Breeze

53. Off the field (init.)

54. Stadium entrances

57. Possible maker of replay screen

60. Logo registration (abbr.)

62. Column heading on roster (abbr.)

63. 3-pointer (init.)

*Solution on page 186*

## RETIRED UNIFORM NUMBERS

Dutch Clark—7

Bobby Layne—22

Doak Walker—37

Joe Schmidt—56

Chuck Hughes—85

Charlie Sanders—88

```
H  A  N  O  S  L  E  I  N  A  D  D  B  S  Y
I  A  O  R  B  M  T  D  I  M  H  C  S  A  E
S  N  N  O  A  A  S  B  T  I  L  L  R  N  N
C  M  X  D  A  U  P  X  H  K  A  R  R  A  S
A  S  I  G  N  M  I  E  O  E  U  G  S  C  G
R  E  N  S  I  O  E  L  M  M  R  H  O  L  T
P  R  L  T  W  F  L  A  P  O  S  X  O  A  L
E  O  A  E  A  F  M  S  S  U  Y  V  L  R  L
R  O  Y  F  L  N  A  V  O  E  E  L  A  K  E
R  M  N  N  K  L  N  B  N  R  N  F  N  M  H
I  X  E  C  E  S  A  S  H  T  R  E  D  N  C
M  T  M  B  R  K  K  Y  E  I  A  I  R  A  T
A  S  E  H  E  S  E  D  A  L  B  I  Y  G  I
N  A  Y  R  E  K  O  R  T  Y  X  O  G  O  M
U  R  O  X  D  N  S  R  E  D  N  A  S  H  G
```

| | | |
|---|---|---|
| BAKER | HAND | MURRAY |
| BARNEY | KARRAS | PERRIMAN |
| BLADES | LANDRY | SANDERS |
| BOX | LAYNE | SCHMIDT |
| CLARK | LEBEAU | SIMS |
| DANIELSON | MAUMOFF | SPIELMAN |
| FARR | MITCHELL | THOMPSON |
| GLOVER | MOORE | WALKER |

# GREEN BAY PACKERS

The Green Bay Packers are the National Football League's version of the New York Yankees and Boston Celtics. They've won 12 NFL championships, more than any other team. They're also one of the most unusual franchises in all of professional sports—sort of what Ben & Jerry's is to ice cream.

The Packers were the first publicly owned franchise in the NFL, and they represent a city that can fit nearly every one of its 100,000 inhabitants into the stadium on a Sunday afternoon.

Men like Curly Lambeau, Don Hutson and Vince Lombardi have made the Packers dominating. Those same men have helped make the Packers unique, too, dating back to the start of the team.

In the summer of 1919, a group of men met in the Green Bay Press-Gazette newspaper office to organize a football team. Lambeau and George Calhoun had come up with the idea a few weeks earlier during a casual street corner conversation and took quick action. Lambeau approached his boss at the Indian Packing Co. about buying some equipment for the team. The company also provided the practice field, so it was natural to refer to the team as "Packers," even when the company sponsorship no longer was needed.

After two highly successful years as an independent team, two executives in the packing plant bought a franchise in the new professional league in 1921. The Packers officially became a pro franchise on Aug. 27, 1921. They defeated the Minneapolis Marines, 7–6, in their first regular season game, and finished the year 3–2–1 in league play. The franchise was reprimanded for using college players under assumed names the following year, but Lambeau promised to obey the rules and bought the franchise for $250 to take control. Poor attendance, brought on in part by bad weather, plagued the team, however, and local merchants raised $2,500 to establish a public, non-profit corporation.

With Lambeau as coach (a position he would hold through 1949), the Packers won their first title in 1929, and followed with two more in a row. They nearly won a fourth the following year when they finished 10–3–1, but Chicago, which had a 7–1–6 record, was awarded the title because ties did not count in the standings.

A freak accident in 1934 nearly caused the franchise to fold. A man fell from the stands, sued and won a $5,000 verdict. The Packers' insurance company went out of business as a result, and the ball club was forced to pay. The franchise didn't have that kind of capital and went into receivership, but a group of Green Bay businessmen raised $15,000 to save the team.

However, that turmoil soon was forgotten with the emergence of Hutson. The end from the University of Alabama was a terror from the start and helped the Packers to three more championships: 1936, '39 and '44. Hutson set an all-time scoring record for one quarter in 1945 when he caught four touchdown passes and kicked five extra points for 29 points in the second period of a game against the Detroit Lions. He retired following that season with 99 touchdown catches, the most in NFL history at the time (he still ranks third overall behind Jerry Rice and Steve Largent). He also led the league in receptions eight years, in receiving yardage seven years, and in scoring five seasons, all records. He was credited with inventing pass patterns, and is still the Packers' all-time scoring leader.

The Packers began a long, slow decline after Hutson's retirement. They bottomed out in 1949 at 2–10. Attendance dropped off so severely that they played an intrasquad game on Thanksgiving Day to raise $50,000 and remain afloat.

More changes were forthcoming in 1950. Lambeau left to become vice president and head coach of the Chicago Cardinals, a stock drive raised $118,000 to put the franchise on a sound financial basis, and the team's colors were changed to green and gold (eliminating navy blue). Later, Lambeau Field was built in time for the 1957 season at a cost of $960,000.

By 1959, the Packers, who hadn't had a winning season since 1947, were desperately searching for the right coach. They selected an assistant coach from the New York Giants with no head coaching experience. His name was Lombardi.

Lombardi's first team went 7–5, and he was named the NFL Coach of the Year. In 1960 the Packers were 8–4 and won the Western Conference title. In 1961, '62, '65, '66 and '67 they won the NFL championship. They also won the first two Super Bowls, in 1966 and '67. Over a nine-year span as head coach, Lombardi's teams were 98–30–4 (.758). Even more remarkable, the Packers were 9–1 in postseason games. The stars were many, including players such as Paul Hornung, Jerry Kramer, Bart Starr, Ray Nitschke, Jim Taylor, Forrest Gregg, Herb Adderley, Jim Ringo, Willie Davis and Willie Wood. Still, Lombardi was successful in enforcing a "team before individual" philosophy.

Following Lombardi's resignation in the spring of 1968, the Packers slid. They still managed to win the National Football Conference's Central Division in 1972, but lost to the Washington Redskins in the playoffs. They tied for the division title in 1978, but didn't qualify for the playoffs. In 1982, a strike-shortened season, they won the division and beat the St. Louis Cardinals in the first round of the playoffs, but lost to the Dallas Cowboys, 37–26, in the second round. They tied for first in their division in 1989, but did not qualify for the playoffs.

Mike Holmgren was hired as the head coach following the 1991 season. The Packers returned to the playoffs as a Wild Card team in 1993 and beat Detroit in the opening round before losing to eventual Super Bowl champion, Dallas, 27–17. Green Bay was back in postseason play in 1994, losing in the division playoffs.

The Packers then began a run of three straight Central Division titles. In 1996, led by league MVP Brett Favre at quarterback and Reggie White at defensive end, the Packers again reigned supreme in the NFL. They won Super Bowl XXXI at New Orleans, beating the New England Patriots, 35–21.

The Packers were back in the Super Bowl the following year, but were upset by the Denver Broncos, 31–24.

*Copyright © 1997 Brian Spurlock/Spurlock Photography, Inc.*

*Brett Favre has thrown for 3,000+ yards in six consecutive seasons.*

## INDIVIDUAL RECORDS

### Career

> Rushing Yards: 8,207, Jim Taylor, 1958–66
> Passing Yards: 24,718, Bart Starr, 1956–71
> Receptions: 595, Sterling Sharpe, 1988–94
> Interceptions: 52, Bobby Dillon, 1952–59
> Touchdowns: 105, Don Hutson, 1935–45
> Points: 823, Don Hutson, 1935–45

### Season

> Rushing Yards: 1,474, Jim Taylor, 1962
> Passing Yards: 4,458, Lynn Dickey, 1983
> Receptions: 112, Sterling Sharpe, 1993
> Interceptions: 10, Irv Comp, 1943
> Touchdowns: 19, Jim Taylor, 1962
> Points: 176, Paul Hornung, 1960

## ACROSS

2. MVP QB

5. 10-yard penalty

9. 2 safeties

10. T-shirt size (abbr.)

13. Edgar Bennett to friends

15. Packers' career scoring leader

17. Prevent a TD

18. Packers' head coach

20. WR Patrick or LB Randy

21. Go ___ it!

23. Packers' leading rusher, 1994–96

26. ___ might go all the way!

27. DB David or T Don

30. Packers' career receiving leader

32. He threw for a team-record 4,458 yards in '83

33. Try a 3-pointer (init.)

34. Name on the championship trophy

36. Column heading on roster (abbr.)

37. 1-on-1 (abbr.)

38. Shoulder, hip or knee

41. No. 5

45. Formation: shot___

46. Sharp turn

48. After John, Hut or Thomp

50. Tied

51. Travis Williams' specialty (init.)

54. Tied NFL record with 4 interceptions in '78 game

57. Years of players

59. Sunday morning activity

60. Post-game pub activity

62. Detroit's time zone (init.)

63. Players' home the night before games

## DOWN

1. Blitz: red___

2. Packers' receiving leader, 1996–97

3. Against (abbr.)

4. Former

6. Oregon CB Muhammad ___

7. Say what?

8. Recovered 20 fumbles from 1958–72

11. ___ Angeles

12. Packers' career leader in receiving yards

14. Meet

16. 1st word of the national anthem

19. Point value of PAT kick

21. Pick up a loose ball (init.)

22. Qtr.

23. Coach's responsibility at hotel after curfew

24. Pain in the ___

25. Packers' career rushing leader

26. Difficult

28. Part of FGA

29. Bad player

30. Packers' QB in Super Bowls I and II

31. Publicity (init.)

33. Yellow hanky

35. Hotel

39. Lower your head

40. Try (abbr.)

41. WR Desmond and B Lynn

42. Before side and after Johns

43. Utilize

44. All-pro became head coach, 1984–87

47. Key time

49. ___-announcer (init.)

52. Regulations

53. Pain

55. Mesh material keeps balls from going into the stands

56. Roaming defensive back (init.)

58. Dine

61. Away

*Solution on page 187*

---

**RETIRED UNIFORM NUMBERS**

Tony Canadeo—3

Don Hutson—14

Bart Starr—15

Ray Nitschke—66

```
O  T  R  W  H  I  T  E  O  T  L  V  L  N  G
M  E  A  O  O  I  T  R  A  E  O  O  O  N  N
G  E  A  Y  F  O  L  E  V  A  F  S  H  I  U
V  N  K  V  L  P  D  E  Y  T  R  S  A  T  N
B  O  O  C  R  O  N  K  O  E  T  T  R  S  R
S  S  I  E  A  S  R  N  D  A  E  J  R  C  O
N  N  I  O  N  J  V  N  R  J  O  G  I  H  H
A  H  S  V  G  L  A  R  C  R  R  C  S  K  A
L  O  M  B  A  R  D  I  D  E  O  T  F  E  I
N  J  R  C  I  D  T  A  G  R  E  M  A  R  K
O  W  G  N  V  L  N  G  E  O  R  P  E  S  O
S  A  G  R  E  Y  L  C  H  I  P  R  Y  O  T
T  O  Y  E  L  R  E  D  D  A  V  N  H  P  E
U  V  C  K  C  I  U  S  M  A  I  L  L  I  W
H  S  H  A  R  P  E  F  F  D  I  C  K  E  Y
```

| | | |
|---|---|---|
| ADDERLEY | HUTSON | NITSCHKE |
| ANDERSON | JACKE | RINGO |
| DAVIS | JOHNSON | SHARPE |
| DICKEY | JORDAN | STARR |
| FAVRE | KRAMER | TAYLOR |
| GREGG | LEVENS | WHITE |
| HARRIS | LOFTON | WILLIAMS |
| HORNUNG | LOMBARDI | WOOD |

# INDIANAPOLIS COLTS

The Indianapolis Colts franchise could be excused for not being quite sure of its heritage. The club has been adopted by new cities several times.

The franchise began as the Miami Seahawks in the old All-America Football Conference. The franchise went bankrupt in 1946 and was relocated to Baltimore by a group of new owners. The nickname was changed to "Colts" and the team colors were green and silver. The Colts finished 2–11–1, then 7–8—which was good enough for a share of the Eastern Division title—and then 1–11. After the 1949 season, they merged into the National Football League with two other AAFC teams. They went 1–11 again in 1950, and finally their ineptitude caught up with them. With few fans still interested in them, they were dissolved by the league after the season because of financial problems.

That franchise, however, was not the forerunner of the one that exists today. There also was a team in the NFL from 1944–48 called the Boston Yanks. It was founded in part by singer Kate Smith and played in Fenway Park. In 1949 the franchise moved to New York and called itself the Bulldogs. It played in the old Polo Grounds. A year later it moved across town to Yankee Stadium and went back to being called the Yanks. In 1952 the Yanks grew tired of competing with the New York Giants and got a better deal in Dallas. They moved south and became known as the Dallas Texans.

Confusing, right? In December of 1952, two years after the old Colts had failed, NFL commissioner Bert Bell went to Baltimore and addressed many of its business leaders. He challenged the city to sell 15,000 season tickets in six weeks. If it did, he promised to bring a franchise back to Baltimore. A week later, the city started selling tickets. In 31 days, it reached the quota. So, Bell had the Texans move to Baltimore and set up Carroll Rosenbloom as the principal owner. The team was renamed the "Colts" and kept the uniform colors—blue and white—that were used in Dallas.

Before the "new" Colts opened play, Baltimore and Cleveland completed one of the largest trades in professional sports history. The Colts received 10 players, including Don Shula, and sent five to the Browns. The changes didn't do much good, though. They were only 3–9 in 1953 and didn't get over .500 until 1957. By then, Weeb Ewbank was the coach, and they had players such as Lenny Moore, Gino Marchetti, Jim Parker, Art Donovan, Raymond Berry and Johnny Unitas.

In 1958 they improved to 9–3 and beat the Giants, 23–17, in the NFL's championship game, in what many fans still call the greatest game ever. The

Colts tied the game at 17 in the final seconds of regulation on a 20-yard field goal by Steve Myhra. Then in sudden-death overtime, Unitas guided the Colts 80 yards in 13 plays, the last one a touchdown dive by Alan Ameche.

Baltimore won the title again in 1959, beating the same Giants, 31–16. The team slipped a bit the next few years, and in 1963 Shula—younger than some of his players—took over as head coach. A year later the Colts were 12–2 and back in the championship game. However, they lost to Cleveland, 27–0. The next three seasons, they were 10–3–1, 9–5 and 11–1–2, yet failed to make the playoffs any year. Then in 1968 they were 13–1 and made their first Super Bowl appearance. The Colts were 18-point favorites to beat the American Football League-champion New York Jets, but the Jets, with brash young quarterback Joe Namath, upset them, 16–7, in Super Bowl III in Miami.

The Colts barely missed the playoffs in 1969, but in '70, following the merger of the NFL and AFL, Baltimore won the American Football Conference's Eastern Division with an 11–2–1 record. The Colts won two playoff games to reach the Super Bowl again. This time they faced the Dallas Cowboys in Miami. The Colts' Jim O'Brien hit a 32-yard field goal with five seconds remaining to give Baltimore a 16–13 win.

The team's heritage took another confusing turn in the summer of 1972. Rosenbloom still owned the Colts, but wanted to own the Los Angeles Rams. Robert Irsay had just purchased the Rams, and was willing to swap. So, Rosenbloom and Irsay traded places in the summer of 1972. The Colts went from last place in 1974 (2–12) to first in '75 (10–4) and won three straight division titles. However, they were back in last again in 1978 and '79 and continued to struggle through the early '80s.

As the losing seasons mounted, attendance dwindled. Finally, in the spring of 1984, Irsay decided to move the team to Indianapolis, which had just built a domed stadium. The team's belongings were loaded into a Mayflower van in the middle of a snowy night and moved to Indiana, where the team was greeted joyfully.

However, the Colts' experiences in Indianapolis haven't been much better. They finished 4–12 in the first season, then 5–11 and 3–13. After acquiring all-pro running back Eric Dickerson in a three-way trade with the Rams and Buffalo Bills during the 1987 season, they made the playoffs with a 9–6 record (and lost in the first round). They followed with a 9–7 record, but gradually slipped back to 1–15 in 1991.

Led by quarterback Jim "Captain Comeback" Harbaugh, the Colts got back into the playoffs as a Wild Card team in 1995 and '96. In 1995 they came within one play of reaching the Super Bowl, losing to the Pittsburgh Steelers, 20–16, in the AFC championship game.

The Colts fell hard in 1997, to 3–13, the worst record in the NFL. That did qualify them, though, for the No. 1 pick in the college draft. For the third time in 15 years, the Colts used the first overall pick on a quarterback, Peyton Manning from the University of Tennessee. The Colts hope that Manning is more productive than the other two selections: John Elway in 1983 (who refused to report and forced the Colts to trade him) and Jeff George in '90 (who was traded after four stormy seasons filled with injuries and a hold-out).

*Copyright © 1995 Brian Spurlock/Spurlock Photography, Inc.*

*Marshall Faulk has played in the Pro Bowl twice.*

## INDIVIDUAL RECORDS

### Career

    Rushing Yards: 5,487, Lydell Mitchell, 1972–77

    Passing Yards: 39,768, Johnny Unitas, 1956–72

    Receptions: 631, Raymond Berry, 1955–67

    Interceptions: 57, Bob Boyd, 1960–68

    Touchdowns: 113, Lenny Moore, 1956–67

    Points: 783, Dean Biasucci, 1984, 1986–94

### Season

    Rushing Yards: 1,659, Eric Dickerson, 1988

    Passing Yards: 3,481, Johnny Unitas, 1963

    Receptions: 85, Reggie Langhorne, 1993

    Interceptions: 11, Tom Keane, 1953

    Touchdowns: 20, Lenny Moore, 1964

    Points: 135, Cary Blanchard, 1996

## ACROSS

1. Surprise
3. Pass pattern
8. Colts' receiving leader in '97
9. Colts' career rushing leader
12. Allow
13. Publicity (init.)
15. Above the stadium
17. Colts' No. 1 draft pick in '97
19. Colts' career receiving leader
20. WR
21. Stomach muscles (abbr.)
22. Colts' stadium sponsor
24. Unit without the ball (abbr.)
28. 2 safeties
30. ___-draft camp
31. Caught team-record 13 passes in '79 game
32. Beside the RG
33. ___ vs. Them
34. 1st and ___
36. ___-captain
40. No. 28
41. Set team-record with 1,659 rushing yards in '88
44. Bernard Whittington's position (init.)
45. Free weekend
46. Help on a tackle
47. Taper
49. Steve Martin's position (init.)

51. Big in stature
53. Tackle the passer
54. Participants
56. S Sims or DT Tabor
59. Blocking from behind
62. Run before throwing the ball
64. Tony Mandarich's position (init.)
65. T-shirt size (abbr.)

## DOWN

1. WR
2. Colts' career passing leader
3. A cheer
4. Stop the ball carrier behind the line (init.)
5. Attempt
6. Block
7. Covers the feet
8. Captain Comeback
9. Fans who belong to a private club
10. Fire
11. Limb
14. Type of x-ray (init.)
16. Column heading on roster
18. Colts' coach, 1996–97

23. Go ___ it!
25. Female Ram
26. ___ away at the lead
27. New Colts coach
29. RB Dick Young's alma mater (init.)
30. Sports bar with darts
35. Action after the snap
37. Extra period
38. Colts' career scoring leader
39. Practice footwear
40. ___ Tarkenton
42. Smooch with your sister after a tie
43. Beside the RG
45. Boast
48. Indianapolis' time zone (init.)
50. Plot
52. Beside the LG
55. Ache
57. Foe (abbr.)
58. Former AFC network
60. Former home of the Raiders (init.)
61. A cheer
63. Former

*Solution on page 187*

---

## RETIRED UNIFORM NUMBERS

Johnny Unitas—19
Buddy Young—22
Lenny Moore—24
Art Donovan—70

Jim Parker—77
Raymond Berry—82
Gino Marchetti—89

```
L  E  I  N  A  D  N  O  S  R  E  K  C  I  D
Y  M  A  Z  T  O  G  E  O  R  G  E  L  D  A
A  A  U  A  E  D  U  R  T  B  A  O  O  O  E
S  R  R  N  I  C  K  O  O  C  G  M  N  N  H
R  C  Y  R  J  F  E  Y  O  A  E  U  D  A  C
I  H  A  R  W  O  D  R  N  W  S  E  A  L  E
I  E  B  S  R  B  N  E  O  T  R  B  L  D  M
C  T  S  E  A  E  T  E  A  O  T  E  L  S  A
C  T  K  E  C  T  B  R  S  E  X  C  L  O  Y
U  I  O  E  A  K  K  K  R  R  H  H  A  N  S
S  M  O  M  N  J  H  O  L  E  E  E  R  O  A
A  L  R  I  R  U  O  B  C  U  R  R  R  N  T
I  C  B  S  D  M  M  M  R  U  A  T  O  N  I
B  H  G  U  A  B  R  A  H  R  E  F  M  A  N
M  I  T  C  H  E  L  L  Y  E  K  C  I  D  U
```

| | | |
|---|---|---|
| AMECHE | DONALDSON | MARCHETTI |
| BERRY | FAULK | MATTE |
| BIASUCCI | GEORGE | MITCHELL |
| BOYD | HARBAUGH | MOORE |
| BROOKS | IRSAY | MORRALL |
| DANIEL | JONES | STARK |
| DICKERSON | LEE | TRUDEAU |
| DICKEY | LOGAN | UNITAS |

# JACKSONVILLE JAGUARS

The idea for a third National Football League franchise in Florida began in 1989 with the forming of Touchdown Jacksonville!, a partnership led by Tom Petway. When NFL Commissioner Paul Tagliabue announced in 1990 that the league was going to expand by two teams, the city of Jacksonville accelerated its efforts.

The city council voted to commit $60 million to renovate the Gator Bowl. The governor signed into law a statute that provided state funds for new facilities. And the local group came up with the necessary money to file an expansion application.

The nickname "Jaguars" was chosen early in the process in a vote of fans. It bested Sharks, Stingrays and Panthers.

However, talks with the city soon bogged down. The organizing committee shut its office and returned ticket deposits when the city failed to approve an increase in costs for stadium renovation. Finally, a compromise was reached and the NFL selected Jacksonville as its 30th franchise on Nov. 30, 1993.

The work continued. Tom Coughlin, the former head coach at Boston College and assistant with the New York Giants, was hired as the Jaguars' coach early in 1994. The club began working out free agents later that year. On Dec. 15 the Jaguars signed 10 players: wide receiver Shannon Baker, linebacker Hillary Butler, defensive end Ferric Collons, offensive lineman Greg Huntington, running back Randy Jordan, defensive end Ernie Logan, offensive tackle Rickie Shaw, defensive end Jason Simmons, defensive end Ricky Sutton and defensive end Chris Williams.

A short time later Dick Jauron was named the defensive coordinator, and Kevin Gilbride was named the offensive coordinator. On Valentine's Day, 1995, the Jaguars drafted 31 players in the expansion draft. The first player selected was quarterback Steve Beuerlein of the Arizona Cardinals. Jacksonville also obtained Desmond Howard, Keith Goganious, Darren Carrington, Reggie Cobb, Eugene Chung and Derek Brown.

The Jaguars added more players through unrestricted free agent signings, then orchestrated their first trade, a day prior to the college draft. Jacksonville obtained quarterback Mark Brunell from the Green Bay Packers in exchange for two draft choices.

Jacksonville used its first pick in the college draft—the second overall pick—for offensive tackle Tony Boselli from the University of Southern California.

With an additional first-round selection, the Jaguars took running back James Stewart from the University of Tennessee.

The Jaguars finally hit the field in the Hall of Fame Game during the preseason. They lost to fellow expansionist, the Carolina Panthers, 20–14. Jacksonville wound up 2–3 in exhibition games, then opened the regular season at home against the Houston Oilers. The Jaguars lost, 10–3, and were beaten in their next three games, also. The team's first victory came at Houston, 17–16, in Week 5. The following week, the Jaguars won again, beating the Pittsburgh Steelers, 20–16. That marked the only time an expansion team has beaten a team that has gone on to play in the Super Bowl.

After a loss against the Chicago Bears, the Jaguars made it three wins in four games with a 23–15 victory over the Cleveland Browns. However, Jacksonville lost its next seven games before winning its finale, 24–21, against Cleveland. Stewart led the team in rushing with 525 yards; Brunell threw for 2,168 yards and 15 touchdowns; Willie Jackson led with 53 catches.

The following season, the Jaguars got little attention by winning just once in the first four games. After 11 weeks, they stood 4–7. A 28–25 overtime victory over the Baltimore Ravens sparked the Jaguars. They followed that with a 30–27 win over the Cincinnati Bengals, then a 23–17 victory against Houston. Jacksonville edged the Seattle Seahawks, 20–13, to set the stage in the final week of the season.

The Jaguars clinched a spot in the playoffs with a 19–17 win over Atlanta as the Falcons' Morten Andersen's 30-yard field goal attempt went wide left on the final play of the game.

As the city of Jacksonville erupted, the coaching staff began plotting strategy for the post-season. First up was a trip to play the Buffalo Bills. Led by Natrone Means' 175 yards on the ground, the Jaguars beat the Bills, 30–27, and became the first team to defeat the Bills in a playoff game in Buffalo's Rich Stadium.

The following week, the Jaguars were heavy underdogs to the Denver Broncos. However, Means ran for another 140 yards and the Jaguars played error-free ball in winning, 30–27. After returning to Jacksonville at 1:30 a.m., the team was greeted by 40,000 fans waiting in the stadium. It was on to the American Football Conference championship game against the New England Patriots.

With a wind-chill of 0 degrees, four Jacksonville turnovers led to 17 points as the Patriots downed the Jaguars, 20–6.

Jacksonville continued its winning ways in 1997. The Jaguars won their first three games and five of the first six. They wound up 11–5, tied for first with Pittsburgh in the AFC's Central Division. Brunell threw for 3,281 yards and 18 TDs; Means ran for 823 yards; Keenan McCardell and Jimmy Smith combined for 167 catches, good for 2,488 yards; Mike Hollis connected on 31–of–36 field goal attempts; Deon Figures had five interceptions; and Clyde Simmons had 8.5 sacks.

In the opening round of the playoffs, the Jaguars had a rematch with the Broncos. This time John Elway led Denver to a 42–17 victory, the first step of the Broncos' run for the Super Bowl title.

Copyright © 1997 Michael C. Hebert/Spurlock Photography, Inc.

*Mark Brunell led the league's QBs in both passing and rushing yards in 1996, a first since 1963.*

## INDIVIDUAL RECORDS

### Career

Rushing Yards: 1,803, James Stewart, 1995–97

Passing Yards: 9,816, Mark Brunell, 1995–97

Receptions: 187, Jimmy Smith, 1995–97

Interceptions: 5, Chris Hudson, 1995–97, and Deon Figures, 1997

Touchdowns: 22, James Stewart, 1995–97

Points: 338, Mike Hollis, 1995–97

### Season

Rushing Yards: 823, Natrone Means, 1997

Passing Yards: 4,367, Mark Brunell, 1996

Receptions: 85, Keenan McCardell, 1996 and 1997

Interceptions: 5, Deon Figures, 1997

Touchdowns: 10, James Stewart, 1996

Points: 134, Mike Holis, 1997

## ACROSS

3. Away
7. Victory
9. Led NFL QBs in passing and rushing yards in '96
10. Coach's title to rookies
11. Jaguars' head coach
12. 1st and ___
13. Jaguars' career rushing leader
15. Utilize
17. Derek Brown's position (init.)
18. Make a mistake
20. Center, guards and tackles (init.)
22. Where severely injured players are sent (init.)
23. List of players
25. One ALLTEL Stadium Place
29. ___-announcer (init.)
30. TD + PAT + FG
31. List for hurt players (init.)
32. Jaguars' career scoring leader
34. Brian DeMarco's alma mater (init.)
36. Effects of sprained ankle
38. Review tape and playbook
39. Had 5 interceptions in '97
41. Against (abbr.)

42. Tony Brackens' alma mater (init.)
44. Whirlpool
46. Lanes
47. Preseason: training ___
48. Sharp turn
49. Spectators
52. Mike Hollis' position (init.)
53. HB in I-formation
54. Failed to tell the truth
57. Possible training table delicacy
58. Foe
60. Beside the RG
62. Precipitation
65. WR
66. Column heading on roster
67. Ducats

## DOWN

1. 4th down kickers
2. Holds Jaguars' record for longest run, 62 yards
3. Jaguars' stadium sponsor
4. Capacity crowd (init.)
5. Stadium level
6. Game spheres
7. Jaguars' '97 No. 1 draft pick
8. On the back of jerseys
9. Jaguars' punter
10. Caught team-record 85 passes in '96 and '97
14. Ripped

16. Former
17. Squads
19. 1st year players
21. Clyde Simmons' position (init.)
24. Makes a shoestring tackle
26. Baseball stat (init.)
27. ___ Petersburg
28. Ready, ___, go!
32. '94 Jim Thorpe Award winner at Colorado
33. Holds team record with 3 TDs in '95 game
35. James Stewart's alma mater (init.)
37. Chosen to All-America Farm Football team in '95
40. Youth baseball teammate of Michael Jordan
41. Win
42. It's ___, it's good!
43. Give-away, ___-away
44. Top player
45. Part of PAT
50. Stomach muscle (abbr.)
51. Angled pass pattern
55. ___ or die
56. Placement of the ball
59. Chris Hudson's home state (abbr.)
61. Pete Mitchell's position (init.)
63. Wire service
64. Make no attempt to return a punt (init.)

*Solution on page 188*

**RETIRED UNIFORM NUMBERS**

None

```
N B R A C K E N S E H R M B W
I P P H I L L E S O B A C E I
S E A R C Y A O L R G O C R D
T S A M O H T L C M L B A C E
N S N R T I I N E E R D R U L
A O E W O S U A M E O R D U L
C E L R U A N A B R B I E S T
B S E O U S N E S N I H L M I
M M M Y C G N M N I N A L E L
B I P R D O I E O L S W R E L
A T I V S R D F M H O O I N E
R H U D A L A N M G N L S G N
K R U Y O L A H I U W R O E U
E H E B R O O K S O C A N F R
R S T E W A R T N C I B L S B
```

| | | |
|---|---|---|
| BARKER | COUGHLIN | ROBINSON |
| BARLOW | FIGURES | SEARCY |
| BOSELLI | HARDY | SIMMONS |
| BRACKENS | HOLLIS | SMEENGE |
| BROOKS | HUDSON | SMITH |
| BRUNELL | MCCARDELL | STEWART |
| COLEMAN | MEANS | THOMAS |
| COLON | RISON | WIDELL |

# KANSAS CITY CHIEFS

**L**amar Hunt made the Kansas City Chiefs one of the most successful franchises in professional football. Some people say Hunt should get the same credit for making the National Football League as successful as it is.

It was Hunt who established and organized the American Football League. He was just three years out of Southern Methodist University, with a degree in geology, when he carried out the idea of starting a rival pro football league. Six cities were represented at that first meeting in the fall of 1959. Hunt grabbed a franchise for Dallas and called it the "Texans." He then hired Hank Stram, an unknown assistant coach at the University of Miami (Fla.), to head his team.

In the inaugural season of 1960, Dallas went 8–6 and finished second in the Western Conference. Texan Abner Haynes led the AFL in rushing with 875 yards. In the 1961 college draft, the Texans selected highly touted center E. J. Holub, but so did the cross-town rival NFL team, the Dallas Cowboys. The Texans won the battle, but the war was still to come. The Texans also acquired future stars Jerry Mays, Fred Arbanas and Jim Tyrer in that draft.

In 1961 the Texans fell to 6–8, but still placed second. Following the season Dallas acquired quarterback Len Dawson, who had spent six uneventful years in the NFL with the Pittsburgh Steelers and Cleveland Browns. Dawson's presence was felt immediately. He was named the league's Player of the Year as the Texans won the 1962 AFL championship. Tommy Brooker hit a 25-yard field goal in the second overtime to give Dallas a win over the Houston Oilers, 20–17.

On May 14, 1963, Hunt announced that the Texans were leaving Dallas (and the Cowboys) and moving to the untapped market of Kansas City. The team became known as the "Chiefs." The Chiefs won their first game in Kansas City, but finished the season 5–7–2. They were 7–7 in 1964, then 7–5–2 in '65.

The Chiefs selected Heisman Trophy winner Mike Garrett, a running back from the University of Southern California, in the 1966 college draft. Garrett ran wild and Dawson led the league in passing for the second time in three years as the Chiefs rolled to an 11–2–1 record. They beat the Buffalo Bills, 31–7, in the AFL championship game and then advanced to the first Super Bowl at the Memorial Coliseum in Los Angeles against the Green Bay Packers. A crowd of 61,000 watched the Packers pull away from the Chiefs in the second half to win, 35–10. The Chiefs were part of history. However, Hunt also left his mark on the Super Bowl. He was the one who gave the championship game its name, getting the idea from the child's toy "Super Ball."

The Chiefs added Willie Lanier, Jim Lynch, Jan Stenerud and Noland Smith and continued their success. They were back in the Super Bowl in 1969 and won it this time, beating the Minnesota Vikings, 23–7, in New Orleans. Dawson was the game's MVP, completing 12-of-17 passes for 142 yards and one touchdown. The Chiefs' defense also excelled during that era. Kansas City led the league in interceptions for a record five consecutive years from 1966–70.

In 1970 the Chiefs merged with the other AFL teams into the NFL. The Texans/Chiefs were the winningest team in the 10-year history of the upstart league, and they continued their winning ways in 1971 by going 10–3–1. In the playoffs, they hooked up with the Miami Dolphins to play the longest game in NFL history. The Chiefs lost to the Dolphins, 27–24, in double overtime, in the final game in old Municipal Stadium.

The Chiefs moved into luxurious Arrowhead Stadium the following year, and Hunt was the first AFL figure inducted into the Pro Football Hall of Fame. The team didn't fare as well on the field, however. Stram and Dawson left after the 1975 season, when the Chiefs finished just 5–9. Kansas City dropped into the cellar with a 2–12 record in 1976, and stayed there for three years. The Chiefs appeared to get over the hump in 1981 with a 9–7 record under Marv Levy, but in 1983 they were back in last place.

Kansas City returned to the playoffs in 1986 after a 10–6 finish behind coach John Mackovic and quarterback Bill Kenney. Mackovic left following the season, and the Chiefs returned to the cellar in 1987 and '88. By then, Steve DeBerg was calling the signals, Christian Okoye was the NFL's leading rusher and Marty Schottenheimer was the head coach. Schottenheimer has established consistency in Kansas City. In his nine seasons there, the Chiefs have finished either first or second in the Western Division each year.

Kansas City improved to 8–7–1 in 1989, then made the playoffs in 1990 with an 11–5 record. The Chiefs were eliminated in the first round by Miami, 17–16. They returned to the playoffs the following year with a 10–6 record. The Chiefs' defense, led by linebacker Derrick Thomas and safety Deron Cherry, forced five Raiders turnovers and held Los Angeles without a touchdown in a 10–6 win in the first round of the playoffs. In the divisional playoffs, Buffalo rolled up a 17–0 halftime lead and defeated the Chiefs, 37–14. The Chiefs made the playoffs again at 10–6 in 1992, but they lost their Wild Card game to the San Diego Chargers, 17–0.

The Chiefs acquired quarterback Joe Montana prior to the 1993 season, and he helped lead the Chiefs to an 11–5 record and back into the playoffs. Kansas City beat the Pittsburgh Steelers, 27–24 in overtime, in the first round, then upset Houston, 28–20, to advance to the American Football Conference title game. However, with Montana injured, the Chiefs lost to Buffalo.

Montana led the Chiefs into the playoffs again in 1994, but they lost to Miami in the first round, 27–17. Montana retired and was replaced by Steve Bono in 1995 and '96. The Chiefs rolled to a 13–3 league-best record in 1995, but were upset by the Indianapolis Colts, 10–7, in the divisional playoffs. The Chiefs finished 9–7 in 1996, but missed the playoffs in a tie-breaker.

In 1997 with Elvis Grbac, Rich Gannon and Billy Joe Tolliver sharing the quarterback position, the Chiefs won their final six regular season games to finish with a 13–3 record, tied for the best in the league. Again, though, the Chiefs were upset, 14–10, in the divisional playoffs, this time to the eventual Super Bowl winners, the Denver Broncos.

*Copyright © 1997 Jay Cribfield/Spurlock Photography, Inc.*

*Elvis Grbac has a career quarterback rating of 82.8.*

## INDIVIDUAL RECORDS

### Career

Rushing Yards: 4,897, Christian Okoye, 1987–92

Passing Yards: 28,507, Len Dawson, 1962–75

Receptions: 416, Henry Marshall, 1976–87

Interceptions: 58, Emmitt Thomas, 1966–78

Touchdowns: 60, Otis Taylor, 1965–75

Points: 1,466, Nick Lowery, 1980–93

### Season

Rushing Yards: 1,480, Christian Okoye, 1989

Passing Yards: 4,348, Bill Kenney, 1983

Receptions: 80, Carlos Carson, 1983

Interceptions: 12, Emmitt Thomas, 1974

Touchdowns: 19, Abner Haynes, 1962

Points: 139, Nick Lowery, 1990

## ACROSS

1. Begins the game
5. Named NFL Man of the Year in '93
8. Armed forces unit with slogan of 31 Down
10. Expected landing time of charter (init.)
11. Derrick Thomas' alma mater (init.)
13. RB Greg, T Dave and RB Mack Lee
14. Chiefs' career receiving leader
18. Li'l Abner scored 5 TDs in a '61 game
20. Go ___ it!
22. Chiefs' leading receiver in '97
25. Chiefs' career rushing leader
28. ___-pom squad
29. Monetary penalty
30. James Hasty's position (abbr.)
33. Chiefs' head coach
36. Free weekend
38. Wire service
40. Jersey label: Made in the ___
42. Donnell Bennett's alma mater
43. Chiefs' career passing leader
45. 6-pointer (abbr.)
46. Everyone
47. ___ and tell
49. Chiefs career scoring leader

51. Allow
53. Beside the RT
54. ___ or die
55. Set Chiefs record with 80 catches in '83
57. Chiefs' kick return specialist
58. Place for a nasal strip
61. On the back of a jersey
62. Delayed running play
63. It's ___, it's good!
64. Foe (abbr.)

## DOWN

2. Squad
3. HB
4. WR
5. Chiefs career leader in receiving yards
6. Points ___ turnovers
7. J.T. was Chiefs' top P.R.
8. Chiefs' original league (init.)
9. Are the Chiefs' colors red, gold and white?
12. Marcus Allen's alma mater (init.)
15. Chiefs' stadium
16. Hold the line
17. Threw for team-record 4,348 yards in '83
19. Away

20. Pick up a loose ball (init.)
21. ___ way or the highway!
23. Go for it: 4th and ___
24. Column heading on roster
26. Down and ___
27. Keep your ___ on the ball
31. ___ all that you can be!
32. Only Michigan QB to lead team to 2 bowl wins
33. Bottom half of practice gear
34. Deflects
35. Intercepted 8 passes in '97
36. Sunny
37. Arm joint
39. ___-announcer (init.)
40. Over or ___ number
41. At
44. Averaged team-record 46.0 yards per punt in '65
48. Chiefs' winningest coach
50. ___dog
52. Illinois DE Don ___
54. Mishandle a pass
55. Pro or ___
56. Miss the postseason: ___-playoff team
59. Podolak or Kelley
60. Former home of the Raiders (init.)

*Solution on page 188*

## RETIRED UNIFORM NUMBERS

Jan Stenerud—3
Len Dawson—16
Abner Haynes—28
Stone Johnson—33

Mack Lee Hill—36
Willie Lanier—63
Bobby Bell—78
Buck Buchanan—86

```
B  R  E  R  Y  T  E  T  T  W  A  B  B  M  P
D  U  E  D  I  L  A  H  I  K  E  L  U  A  O
O  I  L  M  B  Y  A  L  W  L  P  Y  R  Y  D
R  L  A  O  L  I  S  N  L  O  V  R  F  S  O
O  L  S  O  H  O  B  H  I  L  L  R  O  T  L
B  E  R  R  N  U  H  T  T  E  Y  E  R  T  A
I  L  I  F  D  N  H  N  L  R  R  H  D  S  K
N  B  U  D  O  O  E  Y  A  N  O  C  T  O  A
S  S  E  S  M  H  N  T  T  N  R  R  E  Y  L
O  S  W  A  U  C  R  T  E  A  A  D  A  A  L
N  A  S  N  H  E  G  E  P  M  N  H  T  N  I
D  L  T  Y  V  E  T  R  S  U  A  A  C  D  N
N  E  S  T  E  N  E  R  U  D  L  Y  E  U  A
O  A  I  C  O  L  O  A  A  D  O  E  R  B
A  R  B  A  N  A  S  G  T  E  U  S  T  W  L
```

| ARBANAS | HAYES | ROBINSON |
|---------|-------|----------|
| BELL | HILL | RUDNAY |
| BUCHANAN | HOLUB | STENERUD |
| BUDDE | HUNT | STRAM |
| BURFORD | LANIER | TAYLOR |
| CHERRY | LYNCH | THOMAS |
| DAWSON | MAYS | TYRER |
| GARRETT | PODOLAK | WILSON |

# MIAMI DOLPHINS

The "perfect" season. It was 1972 in Miami. The Dolphins were coming off a 10–3–1 season and a loss in Super Bowl VI to the Dallas Cowboys. However, the Dolphins had no idea they would make history by going undefeated and untied, a perfect 14–0. It was the first and last time in National Football League history a team did that.

The lineup was awesome. The offensive stars were quarterback Bob Griese, running backs Larry Csonka and Mercury Morris, wide receiver Paul Warfield, tackle Norm Evans and guard Larry Little. The defensive stars were safeties Jake Scott and Dick Anderson, linebacker Nick Buoniconti and end Bill Stanfill. Don Shula was the head coach.

The season started with wins over the Kansas City Chiefs and Houston Oilers. Then the Dolphins had to score 10 fourth-quarter points to edge the Minnesota Vikings, 16–14. Miami went on to defeat the New York Jets, then had all but beaten the San Diego Chargers when Griese went down with a broken right leg and a dislocated ankle. Backup quarterback Earl Morrall, picked up off waivers earlier that spring, finished the 24–10 Miami victory. With Griese out indefinitely, and a 38-year-old cast-off at quarterback, Dolphin fans weren't overly optimistic for the remainder of the season. However, Shula changed to a predominantly run-oriented offense and relied on a sturdy defense to keep the score close.

Miami came from behind in Week 6 to beat the Buffalo Bills, 24–23, then shut out the Baltimore Colts, 23–0. The Dolphins won at Buffalo, then recorded another shutout, white-washing the New England Patriots, 52–0. They got another fourth-quarter win over the Jets to go 10–0, then beat the St. Louis Cardinals, New England and the New York Giants to set the stage for the season finale at home against Baltimore. Once again, the defense rose to the occasion and shut out the Colts for the second time, 16–0.

Because of the emphasis on the running game, Csonka (1,117) and Morris (1,000) became the first teammates to rush for 1,000 yards in the same season. The Dolphins set an NFL rushing record (since broken) with 2,960 yards. Morrall, the quarterback nobody wanted eight months before, completed 55 percent of his passes for 1,360 yards and 11 touchdowns, and threw just seven interceptions.

In the playoffs, the Dolphins again came from behind in the fourth quarter to eliminate the Cleveland Browns, 20–14. Then in the American Football Conference championship game against the Pittsburgh Steelers, Griese came off the bench in the third quarter of a 7–7 game and led the Dolphins to a 21–17 victory. In Super Bowl VII at Memorial Coliseum in Los Angeles, the Dolphins' defense played an almost perfect game to wind up the perfect season. Miami built a 14–0 halftime lead and then held on for a 14–7 win over the Washington Redskins. The Redskins' only touchdown came after kicker Garo Yepremian muffed the ball on a misplayed field goal attempt and tried to pass it. Washington's Mike Bass picked up the ball and returned it 49 yards for a touchdown with 2:07 left in the game. Scott, who had two interceptions, was named the game's Most Valuable Player.

The Dolphins' dominance continued in 1973. They finished 12–2 and beat the Oakland Raiders, 27–10, for their third straight AFC championship. They made it two straight Super Bowl wins with a 24–7 victory over Minnesota.

Miami didn't return to the Super Bowl again until the 1982 season. The Dolphins had a 17–10 halftime lead over Washington on a 76-yard touchdown pass from quarterback David Woodley to wide receiver Jimmy Cefalo and a Super Bowl-record 98-yard kickoff return by Fulton Walker. However, the Redskins took control in the second half and won, 27–17.

The Dolphins were back in the Super Bowl two years later, a season in which they set an NFL record by scoring 70 touchdowns. Miami rode the record-breaking arm of young quarterback Dan Marino (5,084 yards) to go 14–2 in the regular season. The Dolphins defeated the Seattle Seahawks and Pittsburgh in the playoffs, then faced the San Francisco 49ers in Super Bowl XIX. The Dolphins lost, 38–16. Miami won its division again in 1985, '92 and '94, but was beaten in the playoffs each time prior to the Super Bowl.

In 1993 with Marino missing almost the entire season with an injury, Shula made history with his 325th career win. On Nov. 14, the Dolphins and Shula beat the Philadelphia Eagles, 19–14, to break George Halas' record of 324 wins. Miami won nine of its first 11 games, but lost the final five games to miss the playoffs.

The Dolphins came into existence in 1965 when Minneapolis lawyer Joseph Robbie met with American Football League commissioner Joe Foss. Robbie was advised to apply for an expansion team in Miami. After Robbie met with the mayor of Miami, Robbie and television star Danny Thomas made a formal application and were granted the AFL's first expansion franchise. The price tag was $7.5 million.

George Wilson was the team's first coach when the Dolphins began playing in 1966. Miami was 3–11 the first year, but continued to improve and made the playoffs in 1970, Shula's first season as head coach. A year later they were in the Super Bowl against Dallas.

Following the 1993 season, H. Wayne Huizenga bought the Dolphins from the Robbie family. Three years later Shula stepped down as coach and was replaced by Jimmy Johnson.

*Copyright © 1997 Michael C. Hebert/Spurlock Photography, Inc.*

*Dan Marino holds 24 NFL regular season records and is tied for seven others.*

## INDIVIDUAL RECORDS

### Career

    Rushing Yards: 6,737, Larry Csonka, 1968–74, 1979

    Passing Yards: 55,416, Dan Marino, 1983–97

    Receptions: 550, Mark Clayton, 1983–92

    Interceptions: 35, Jake Scott, 1970–75

    Touchdowns: 82, Mark Clayton, 1983–92

    Points: 830, Garo Yepremian, 1970–78

### Season

    Rushing Yards: 1,258, Delvin Williams, 1978

    Passing Yards: 5,084, Dan Marino, 1984

    Receptions: 86, Mark Clayton, 1988

    Interceptions: 10, Dick Westmoreland, 1967

    Touchdowns: 18, Mark Clayton, 1984

    Points: 124, Pete Stoyanovich, 1992

## ACROSS

1. San Jose CB Gerald ___
4. Qtr.
6. Goes around end to block
9. Mercury
10. Turn sharply
11. Dolphins' career rushing leader
13. Usual day off from practice (abbr.)
15. NFL's all-time winningest coach
17. Ran for a team-record 1,258 yards in '78
18. Away
19. A cheer
20. Don't move

21. Was victorious
23. Set team record with 217 yards in receptions in '85 game
25. Do the Dolphins play their home games on grass?
27. Where severely injured players are sent (init.)
29. Stadium signage
30. Direction to New York from Miami
33. Boston U. QB/WR/RB from 1981–92
34. Center, guards and tackles (init.)
35. Treats an ankle sprain
37. Foe (abbr.)

40. TD + PAT
42. Karim
44. Team physician (abbr.)
45. Byron Morris' nickname
46. Dolphins' long-time AFL foe
48. WR
50. Expected landing time of charter (init.)
51. Outscore the opposition
53. Pool stick
55. Garo
57. Dine
59. ___ and 10
61. O.J.
62. Painting or sculpture
63. Former

## DOWN

2. Protected by plastic formed piece
3. Beside the LG
4. Dolphins' stadium
5. Before season and game
6. Area for linemen
7. ___ vs. Them
8. ___ of scrimmage
9. NFL's all-time passing leader
11. Dolphins' career receiving leader
12. Dolphins' punter
13. Logo registration (abbr.)
14. Native country of Kirby Dar Dar (init.)
15. Dolphins' career leader in FG
16. It's ___, it's good!
19. No. 12
22. On the back of a jersey
24. 4th down kicker
26. Holds the line
28. Beside the RG
31. Do ___ die
32. RB Eddie, S Barry or WR Randal
36. Back-up players
38. Set a Dolphins record with 4 TD catches in '73 game
39. Fruit drink
40. Make last-ditch stop at touchdown
41. Column heading on roster
43. College class of early entry draftee (abbr.)
44. Daniel Stubbs' position (init.)
45. Quarter, half and full
47. List for hurt players (init.)
48. Injured: On the ___
49. At
52. Down and ___
54. ___-announcer (init.)
56. Block
58. Mesa WR, 1990–93 (init.)
59. Pick up a loose ball (init.)
60. Troy Dayton's position (init.)

*Solution on page 189*

---

**RETIRED UNIFORM NUMBER**

Bob Griese—12

```
O  Y  L  L  C  H  C  Y  R  E  G  N  A  L  J
M  E  O  O  L  N  O  S  R  E  D  N  A  S  E
H  P  N  Y  A  W  A  R  F  I  E  L  D  T  N
A  R  O  Y  Y  R  A  R  U  P  A  H  T  O  S
R  E  S  J  T  P  C  E  O  T  O  O  R  Y  E
D  M  N  A  O  E  E  O  U  B  C  L  S  A  N
Y  I  E  C  N  R  N  C  I  S  Y  V  E  N  S
O  A  H  K  E  E  I  F  F  U  D  C  M  O  E
N  N  P  S  N  A  I  L  M  S  O  D  E  V  K
A  E  E  O  T  E  L  O  T  N  A  L  R  I  A
M  L  T  N  S  R  O  U  I  U  T  O  I  C  K
W  T  S  E  Y  R  O  R  H  T  P  C  D  H  N
E  S  I  A  E  F  A  C  I  S  K  A  W  T  O
N  R  B  V  F  M  W  L  K  M  O  R  R  I  S
G  K  U  E  C  H  E  N  B  E  R  G  H  W  C
```

| | | |
|---|---|---|
| ANDERSON | KUECHENBERG | ROBY |
| CLAYTON | LANGER | SCOTT |
| CSONKA | LITTLE | SHULA |
| GRIESE | MARINO | STEPHENSON |
| HARDY | MCDUFFIE | STOYANOVICH |
| JACKSON | MOORE | STROCK |
| JENSEN | MORRIS | WARFIELD |
| KIICK | NEWMAN | YEPREMIAN |

# MINNESOTA VIKINGS

The Minnesota Vikings have aroused mixed feelings from their fans. On one hand, they have reached the Super Bowl four times, an impressive accomplishment. On the other hand, they lost all four of those games.

Minnesota was granted an expansion franchise in January 1960. The nickname "Vikings" was selected because of historical ties believed to exist between the original Vikings and the area, as well as the Nordic and Scandinavian ancestry of many of the local residents.

Bert Rose was the first general manager and Norm Van Brocklin the first coach. Fran Tarkenton was the starting quarterback for the Vikings when they finally began play in the 1961 season. They won their opener over the Chicago Bears, 37–13, but then lost seven straight and finished the season 3–11.

Minnesota dropped to 2–11–1 in its second season, but improved to 5–8–1 in 1963. Tommy Mason was an all-pro halfback that season, and kicker Fred Cox began his 15-year career as a Viking.

Minnesota recorded its first winning record (8–5–1) in 1964, tying for second place in the Western Conference, but slipped back the next three seasons. In 1967 Bud Grant was hired to replace Van Brocklin while Tarkenton was shipped to the New York Giants for three draft picks. The Vikings installed the unorthodox Joe Kapp at quarterback. His passes didn't spiral, and he didn't stay in the passing pocket long, but he soon convinced everyone he was a winner.

The Vikings won their division in 1968 with an 8–6 record and made the playoffs for the first time, then stunned the National Football League the following season by producing a league-best 12–2 record. The defense, dubbed "The Purple People Eaters," led the way. Anchored by linemen Alan Page, Carl Eller and Jim Marshall, and safety Paul Krause, the Vikings held their opponents to fewer than 10 points a game. They beat the Los Angeles Rams and Cleveland Browns in the playoffs to advance to Super Bowl IV in New Orleans, but committed five turnovers and lost to the Kansas City Chiefs, 23–7.

Gary Cuozzo replaced Kapp at quarterback in 1970, but the defense remained intact. The Vikings were just as dominant and rolled to another 12–2 record, but were upset by the San Francisco 49ers, 17–14, in the divisional playoffs.

The Vikings won their division for the fourth straight year the following season, but again were upset in the divisional playoffs, this time by the Dallas

Cowboys, 20–12. Page was named the NFL's Most Valuable Player, a rare feat for a defensive lineman. In 1972 Minnesota re-acquired Tarkenton in exchange for three players and two draft choices, but the Vikings slipped to 7–7. They selected running back Chuck Foreman from the University of Miami (Fla.) in the first round of the 1973 college draft, and his presence was felt immediately. He rushed for a team-high 801 yards, was named the NFL Rookie of the Year and was selected to play in the Pro Bowl. The Vikings returned to the top of the National Football Conference's Central Division with a 12–2 record and were back in the Super Bowl. However, Minnesota allowed Miami to score the first two times the Dolphins had the ball, and lost, 24–7.

The Vikings went on to win (or tie for) the division title six straight years. The scrambling Tarkenton, despite his age, continued to get better and better and was the league's MVP in 1975. Foreman became the premier running back in the league, and the defense remained among the stingiest.

Minnesota returned to the Super Bowl following the 1974 season, but lost to the Pittsburgh Steelers, 16–6. Two seasons later the Vikings were in the Super Bowl for the fourth time in eight years, but lost again, to the Oakland Raiders, 32–14. The team was broken up after the 1978 season. Tarkenton retired as the NFL's all-time leader in touchdown passes, completions, attempts and yardage. Page went to the Chicago Bears and Eller to the Seattle Seahawks. A year later, Krause retired and Foreman went to the New England Patriots. The Vikings were 7–9 in 1979, then shared the division title (for the 11th time in 13 years) in 1980.

The continued departures of star players soon caught up with the Vikings, however. They struggled to stay in the middle of the pack until 1987. By then Grant was gone. He retired to the front office in 1984, but returned to the sidelines for one more year after Les Steckel coached the team to a 3–13 record in 1984. Jerry Burns, a longtime assistant, took over in 1986.

Minnesota was a Wild Card playoff team in 1987 and surprised the New Orleans Saints, 44–10, and San Francisco, 36–24, to reach the NFC championship game, but lost there to the Washington Redskins, 17–10. The Vikings were again a Wild Card team the following year. They beat the Los Angeles Rams, 28–17, then lost to San Francisco in the second round, 34–9.

In 1989 the Vikings returned to their glory days and tied for the division title, but lost in the playoffs to San Francisco, 41–13. Minnesota slipped to 6–10 in 1990, and went 8–8 in 1991. Rookie coach Dennis Green guided the Vikings back to the top of the division in 1992 with an 11–5 record, but they were eliminated in the first round of the playoffs by Washington, 24–7. In 1993, the Vikings were back in the playoffs with a 9–7 mark, but lost in the opening round to the New York Giants, 17–10.

Minnesota won its division again in 1994, but were upset by Chicago, 35–18, in the first round of the playoffs. After the Vikings missed postseason play in 1995 with an 8–8 record, Minnesota qualified in '96 and '97. The Vikings lost in the first round to Dallas, 40–15, in 1996; they beat the Giants, 23–22, in the opening round in '97, only to lose to San Francisco, 38–22, in the second round.

*Copyright © 1997 Jay Cribfield/Spurlock Photography, Inc.*

*Cris Carter is the Viking's all-time career receptions leader.*

## INDIVIDUAL RECORDS

### Career

    Rushing Yards: 5,879, Chuck Foreman, 1973–79

    Passing Yards: 33,098, Fran Tarkenton, 1961–66, 1972–78

    Receptions: 667, Cris Carter, 1990–97

    Interceptions: 53, Paul Krause, 1968–79

    Touchdowns: 76, Bill Brown, 1962–74

    Points: 1,365, Fred Cox, 1963–77

### Season

    Rushing Yards: 1,266, Robert Smith, 1997

    Passing Yards: 4,264, Warren Moon, 1994

    Receptions: 122, Cris Carter, 1994 and 1995

    Interceptions: 10, Paul Krause, 1975

    Touchdowns: 22, Chuck Foreman, 1975

    Points: 132, Chuck Foreman, 1975, and Fuad Reveiz, 1994

## ACROSS

1. 43.4 yds., 4.5 avg. or 4-for-5 (abbr.)
6. ___ vs. Them
10. Moore's name change
11. Skein
14. Game's star
16. Away
19. Arm joints
21. Go ___ guy
22. Fran
26. Ref's relative
27. Muscle relaxer: ___ bath
28. DE Carl and family
30. TV talk: Hi, ___!
31. Former Charger QB
33. Publicity (init.)
34. Stadium signage
35. Set team record with 1,266 yards rushing in '97
36. Vikings' leading rusher, 1985–88
38. DT Jerry Shay's alma mater (init.)
39. ___ or under number
41. LB Dennis Johnson's alma mater (init.)
42. USC S recovered team-record 3 fumbles in '85 game
46. ___-announcer (init.)
47. Plead
49. All-pro DT had a brother play with Tampa Bay

51. G.M. for 2 Super Bowl teams
53. ___ all that you can be!
54. Go deep! pass pattern
56. Herschel
57. Fruit drink
59. Type of x-ray (init.)
60. Referee's equipment
64. Free weekend
65. Best ever

## DOWN

1. Usual game day (abbr.)
2. Knot
3. RB Bill, LB Richard and RB Ted
4. Against (abbr.)
5. DT was part of Purple People Eaters
7. DB who covers the TE
8. Afternoon beverage break
9. Scott Sisson's position (abbr.)
12. Shower snapper
13. Try
15. HB
17. Vikings career receiving leader
18. Vikings career rushing leader
20. Dixon Edwards' position (abbr.)
23. Vikings' career interceptions leader
24. Sick
25. Threw for team-record 490 yards in '86 game
29. QB was HS teammate of Brad Daugherty
30. Tulane RB led Vikings in rushing in 1962–63
31. One-third of a yd.
32. Former LB became player personnel coordinator
33. Qtr.
36. Neither rain ___ snow will prevent a game in the Dome
37. 4th Super Bowl
40. Former
42. Game sphere
43. Caught passes for a team-record 210 yards in '76 game
44. HBS
45. Vikings' head coach
48. Vikings' winningest head coach
50. LB tied team record with 3 interceptions in '93 game
52. 1st play of every game (abbr.)
53. Deflect a kick (init.)
54. Go ___ it!
55. OT played 15 seasons from 1968–82
58. Block
60. Column heading on roster
61. Former home of the Raiders (init.)
62. Play ___ or trade me!
63. 6-pointer (abbr.)

*Solution on page 189*

## RETIRED UNIFORM NUMBERS

Fran Tarkenton—10

Alan Page—88

```
E  L  D  N  A  R  K  G  I  L  L  I  A  M  N
K  A  H  F  Y  R  N  O  R  O  S  A  A  A  P
A  X  A  O  A  R  R  O  A  N  E  L  S  O  N
L  P  O  M  T  W  R  I  S  R  K  A  R  M  O
L  H  E  C  A  I  S  R  H  N  A  V  Y  A  F
E  R  I  V  R  N  E  E  A  D  H  A  G  R  E
N  U  E  W  R  S  P  L  D  A  R  O  R  S  S
N  N  I  O  R  T  A  L  W  Y  R  R  J  H  K
E  N  O  F  F  O  H  E  L  G  N  I  T  A  R
C  D  U  O  K  N  E  A  S  M  I  T  H  L  A
A  M  E  A  M  L  N  L  C  V  A  D  E  L  U
R  A  P  U  G  W  I  C  E  T  I  H  W  C  S
T  P  R  O  O  A  L  L  E  W  D  U  T  S  E
E  F  O  R  E  M  A  N  H  S  O  V  U  O  V
R  R  B  W  A  M  T  A  R  K  E  N  T  O  N
```

| | | |
|---|---|---|
| ALLEN | JOHNSON | RASHAD |
| BROWN | KAPP | SMITH |
| CARTER | KRAMER | STUDWELL |
| COX | KRAUSE | TARKENTON |
| ELLER | MARSHALL | TINGLEHOFF |
| FOREMAN | MOON | WHITE |
| GILLIAM | NELSON | WINSTON |
| IRWIN | RANDLE | YARY |

# NEW ENGLAND PATRIOTS

**F**ew professional football franchises have experienced highs and lows as the New England Patriots have. In 1985, for example, the Patriots were the Cinderella team of the National Football League. They had been a respectable 9–7 in 1984 when Raymond Berry began his first full year as the head coach after replacing Ron Meyer midway through the previous season. Tony Eason proved he was a reliable quarterback that season, and Craig James was a steady runner. The offensive line was very good, anchored by guard John Hannah and tackle Brian Holloway. The defense was led by linebackers Steve Nelson and Andre Tippett and defensive backs Ray Clayborn and Fred Marion.

However, the 1985 season started slowly for the Patriots. They beat the Green Bay Packers in the opener, but lost three of their next four games to drop to 2–3. Finally, things began to come together. New England won six games in a row, lost, then won three of its final four games to finish 11–5. It took a win on the last day of the regular season to secure the final Wild Card playoff spot. Just four years earlier, the Patriots had the worst record (2–14) in the league. Now they were going to the playoffs.

As the last Wild Card team in the playoffs, the Patriots had to play their opening game on the road, and would have to play each game thereafter away from home as well. The Patriots were well aware that no team in the history of the NFL had won three road games to advance to the title game. It just wasn't done.

They beat the Jets in New York, 26–14, then traveled to Los Angeles to play the Raiders, who had won the American Football Conference's Western Division with a 12–4 record. The Patriots won again, 27–20. Game 3 was in Miami for the AFC championship and the right to play in the Super Bowl. The Patriots had lost at Miami, 30–27, during the regular season, and had lost 18 straight games there, winning only in 1966. Miami was a heavy favorite, but the Patriots won again, 31–14.

Next up, the Super Bowl. Unfortunately, the good part of the story for the Patriots ends there. They were crushed by the Chicago Bears, 46–10, in New Orleans' Superdome, the largest margin of victory (at the time) in Super Bowl history. New England took the quickest lead in Super Bowl history after Larry McGrew recovered a fumble on Chicago's 19-yard line. Tony Franklin later kicked a 36-yard field goal with just 1 minute, 19 seconds elapsed in the game. The Bears went on to take a 23–3 halftime lead, and held the Patriots to just seven yards rushing for the game.

Still, the Patriots were regaled as underdogs who had overcome the odds. The telecast of that game was the most-watched program in history at the time. With 127 million viewers in the U.S., it surpassed the final episode of *M*A*S*H*. The game also was televised in 59 foreign countries and was seen by an estimated 300 million Chinese on a tape delay.

The high of that season was followed by some deep lows, however. In 1990 the Patriots finished 1–15. Two years later they lost their first nine games before winning at Indianapolis. With coach Dick MacPherson in the hospital and third-string quarterback Scott Zolak—a former water boy for Joe Montana's high school team—calling the plays, the Patriots beat the Colts, 37–34, in overtime. They won again the following week, this time over the New York Jets, 24–3. However, the Patriots lost their final five games to finish 2–14. They were shut out three times, and attendance at home games fell as low as 19,429.

The Patriots always have been a team of highs and lows. They started as the Boston Patriots in the first American Football League season in 1960. They finished last in their division in the inaugural season. By 1963 they were division champs—with prominent politician-to-be Jack Kemp at quarterback—but lost in the AFL title game to the San Diego Chargers, 51–10. By 1967 they were back in last place. Running back Gino Cappelletti provided many highlights through good times and bad. He finished as the AFL's all-time leading scorer with 1,100 points. Cappelletti, who also kicked, set the team's single-game record for field goals with six in 1964.

The team moved into a new stadium in Foxboro, Mass., for the 1971 season and became known as the New England Patriots. They struggled to stay out of the basement, but in 1976 tied for the American Football Conference's Eastern Division title with an 11–3 mark. They lost in the final 10 seconds of the first-round playoff game that year to the eventual Super Bowl champion Oakland Raiders, 24–21.

The Patriots tied for the division title again in 1978, but lost in the playoffs to the Houston Oilers, 31–14. By 1981, however, they were back in last place. They followed the Super Bowl season of 1985 with a division championship in '86, but lost in the first round of the playoffs.

Hopes for another rebound from the dismal 1992 season were high in 1993. Bill Parcells, who coached the New York Giants to two Super Bowl titles, was hired as head coach, and the Patriots chose promising Washington State University quarterback Drew Bledsoe with the first pick in the draft. The Patriots even changed their uniform and helmet design to accentuate the new look. Running back Jon Vaughn, who led the NFL in kickoff returns in 1992 with a 28.2-yard average, also figured to be a key player. Even with all that hope, the Patriots started the season 1–11.

The Patriots were back in the playoffs in 1994, out in '95, then won the Eastern Division title in '96 (11–5). The Patriots beat the Pittsburgh Steelers, 28–3, in the divisional playoffs, then downed the Jacksonville Jaguars, 20–6, in the AFC championship game to return to the Super Bowl. However, the up-and-down Patriots were beaten by the Green Bay Packers, 35–21, in New Orleans.

Parcells left as the coach following the Super Bowl. He was replaced by Pete Carroll and the fans could have been excused if they figured it was time for the Patriots to drop to the bottom—again. Led by Bledsoe's 3,706 passing yards, Curtis Martin's 1,160 yards on the ground and a defense that registered 43 quarterback sacks (Chris Slade had nine and Henry Thomas seven), the Patriots again won their division. They beat Miami, 17–3, in the opening round of the playoffs, but then lost to the Pittsburgh Steelers, 7–6.

Copyright © 1997 Brian Spurlock/Spurlock Photography, Inc.

*Drew Bledsoe has thrown for more than 18,000 yards in his first five seasons.*

## INDIVIDUAL RECORDS

### Career

    Rushing Yards: 5,453, Sam Cunningham, 1973–79, 1981–82

    Passing Yards: 26,886, Steve Grogan, 1975–90

    Receptions: 534, Stanley Morgan, 1977–89

    Interceptions: 36, Raymond Clayborn, 1977–89

    Touchdowns: 68, Stanley Morgan, 1977–79

    Points: 1,130, Gino Cappelletti, 1960–70

### Season

    Rushing Yards: 1,487, Curtis Martin, 1995

    Passing Yards: 4,555, Drew Bledsoe, 1994

    Receptions: 96, Ben Coates, 1994

    Interceptions: 11, Ron Hall, 1964

    Touchdowns: 17, Curtis Martin, 1996

    Points: 155, Gino Cappelletti, 1964

## ACROSS

1. Foe (abbr.)

3. Set team record with 212 yards rushing in '83 game

6. T-shirt size

9. Intercepted 6 passes in '97

10. Delayed running play

14. Patriots' leading rusher, 1995–97

15. At

17. Beyond LT

18. MNF network

19. No postseason: ___-playoff team

20. Weep

23. Pick-off a pass (abbr.)

24. Adam Vinatieri's position (init.)

25. Patriots' head coach

26. Before side or after Johns

27. ___-announcer (init.)

29. Was ahead

31. Patriots' career passing leader

33. Ben Coates' position (init.)

35. QB threw 179 consecutive passes without an INT in '95

36. Yellow hanky

38. Allow

40. 3–3 or 21–21

41. Patriots' career receiving leader

43. Reveal

44. Jimmy Hitchcock's alma mater's nickname: ___ Heels
45. Column heading on roster
47. ___ or die
49. Mike Bartrum's position (init.)
50. ___ Louis
51. Guard, tackle and end
53. LB has recorded 38.5 sacks in last 5 years
55. Over or ___ number
56. Top player
58. Part of foot kicking the ball
59. Next to the RT
61. ___-captain
63. Arm joint
66. Official's equipment
67. Clock operator
68. Observe

## DOWN

1. Patriots' punter, 1994–95
2. Shoulder, hip and knee
3. Patriots' career interceptions leader
4. Next to the LG
5. Down and ___
6. Patriots' 1st coach
7. ___ way or the highway!
8. Tommy Hodson's alma mater (init.)
9. Patriots' career rushing leader

11. Babe
12. 4.5 yds. or 56.7%
13. Quarter, half or full
16. Column heading on roster
21. Do the Patriots play in Foxboro Stadium?
22. Coach of Patriots in most recent Super Bowl appearance
24. 1 sheet of paper in the playbook
27. Cooking equipment
28. Back-up player
30. Unit without the ball
32. Set a team record with 12 catches in '94 game
34. Away
37. Part of FGA
38. Former home of the Rams (init.)
39. A lineman
40. Bottom of a sneaker
42. Cappelletti
46. Extra session (abbr.)
48. Unit with the ball
52. Star of the game
54. Pull the ball away
57. Evaluate
58. Ball props
62. Ouch!
64. Monty Brown's position (abbr.)
65. Column heading on roster (abbr.)

*Solution on page 190*

## RETIRED UNIFORM NUMBERS

Steve Grogan—14

Gino Cappelletti—20

Mike Haynes—40

Steve Nelson—57

John Hannah—73

Jim Hunt—79

Bob Dee—89

```
M  R  S  E  T  A  O  C  B  L  E  D  S  O  E
A  A  A  L  E  G  N  O  R  T  S  M  R  A  E
R  E  S  E  M  A  J  L  O  S  I  V  R  A  L
I  C  A  D  A  M  S  L  S  V  O  A  S  V  A
O  N  T  T  E  P  P  I  T  T  Y  O  C  I  I
N  A  C  R  N  K  O  N  I  R  N  M  A  R  T
M  N  K  P  I  O  S  S  F  U  P  U  T  A  T
N  S  C  U  T  H  A  N  N  A  H  L  V  E  E
A  S  O  M  R  N  T  T  E  K  N  U  L  P  L
G  T  R  R  A  N  C  H  G  R  N  O  I  B  L
R  A  B  G  M  S  A  K  O  U  O  R  E  S  E
O  N  O  W  D  L  T  F  O  O  S  B  R  A  P
M  R  T  X  L  E  E  T  I  L  L  I  R  A  P
G  N  R  O  B  Y  A  L  C  N  E  D  T  S  A
C  U  N  N  I  N  G  H  A  M  N  I  R  O  C
```

| | | |
|---|---|---|
| ADAMS | CUNNINGHAM | MARTIN |
| ARMSTRONG | EASON | MORGAN |
| BLEDSOE | FRYAR | NANCE |
| BROCK | GROGAN | NELSON |
| CAPPELLETTI | HALL | PARILLI |
| CLAYBORN | HANNAH | PLUNKETT |
| COATES | JAMES | TATUPU |
| COLLINS | MARION | TIPPETT |

# NEW ORLEANS SAINTS

The New Orleans Saints own the dubious distinction of playing the most seasons before registering their first winning season. The franchise was founded in 1967, but the team's fans had to endure 21 seasons before the Saints finally produced a winning record in 1987.

Once the Saints discovered a winning formula, it became contagious—for awhile that is. After seven consecutive seasons of .500+ records, the Saints returned to their losing ways. The last four years the Saints have finished last in their division twice and below .500 two other times.

The road from wretched to respectable was long and painful. Three men were primarily responsible for the transformation. First, there was owner Tom Benson. Then, there was president/general manager Jim Finks. And last, but not least, head coach Jim Mora.

The animated Benson wasn't always a football fan. He was a successful auto dealer living in New Orleans for many years, with little interest in the local football team. However, in 1984, when he heard the Saints were for sale and might leave the Crescent City, he became a concerned citizen. He formed a group of businessmen, and on May 31, 1985, ownership of the Saints was transferred to Benson and his partners for $70 million.

On Jan. 14, 1986, Benson hired Finks, who was responsible for building the Minnesota Vikings and rebuilding the Chicago Bears into championship teams. He also was general manager of the Chicago Cubs in 1984 when they won their first baseball pennant in modern times.

Two weeks later, Benson and Finks hired Mora. He had been the most successful coach in the United States Football League with a 48–13–1 record in three seasons at Philadelphia and Baltimore. His philosophy is simple, as stated by a plaque in his office that reads, "The secret of a good organization is good organization."

The first season the trio was together, the Saints improved by two games to 7–9. The next year, 1987, the Saints recorded their first winning season with a 12–3 record. That was the second-best record in the National Football League, but the Saints had the misfortune of playing in the same division as the San Francisco 49ers, which had the best record. The Saints qualified for the playoffs as a Wild Card team, but lost in the first round to the Minnesota Vikings, 44–10. Six players were voted to the Pro Bowl team that season: kicker Morten Andersen, tight end Hoby Brenner, guard Brad Edelman, running back Rueben Mayes, linebacker Sam Mills and cornerback Dave

Waymer. Mora was named the NFL Coach of the Year and Finks the NFL Executive of the Year.

New Orleans tied for the division title in 1988 with a 10–6 record, but missed the playoffs because of a tie-breaker. It finished 9–7 the next year, but missed the playoffs again. A month into the 1990 season, the Saints traded three draft choices to the Dallas Cowboys for quarterback Steve Walsh. The former No. 1 pick made his first appearance with the Saints on Oct. 14 and completed 15-of-26 passes for 243 yards and three touchdowns. However, a week later, running back Dalton Hilliard, the top touchdown scorer in the league the year before, was lost for the remainder of the season with a knee injury. The Saints still won three of their final four games to finish 8–8 and earn the final Wild Card spot in the playoffs, but lost to the Chicago Bears, 16–6.

The Saints finally won their division outright in 1991 with an 11–5 record. They were led by their defense, which placed three linebackers—Mills, Vaughan Johnson and Pat Swilling—as starters in the Pro Bowl, the most ever from one team. The Saints, however, were upset in the first round of the playoffs by the Atlanta Falcons, 27–20.

New Orleans started the 1992 season 2–2, but finished the year 12–4. The Saints qualified for the playoffs for the fourth time in six years, but again lost in the first round, this time to the Philadelphia Eagles, 36–20. In 1993, the Saints missed the playoffs for the first time in four years with an 8–8 record.

Things began to change dramatically for the Saints. Finks became ill and died. Mora resigned midway through the 1996 season. Bill Kuharich took over as president and general manager of the team; at age 44, he is the youngest chief operating officer in the NFL. Former Bears mentor Mike Ditka was hired as head coach prior to the 1997 season. Only Benson remains in the same position from the winning days.

Although New Orleans is winless in postseason play, many of its fans can recall much darker days. The Saints entered the NFL as an expansion team in 1967. They were 3–11 that first season and couldn't win more than five games a season through the first 11 years. They improved to 7–9 in 1978 and then to 8–8, but tumbled to 1–15 in 1980 and stayed down until the arrival of Benson, Finks and Mora.

The Saints did produce one historic moment in those early years. Tom Dempsey, a kicker born without a portion of his kicking foot, kicked a game-winning 63-yard field goal in 1970, a league record that still stands. Another notable event was the 1975 opening of the Superdome, the largest indoor stadium in the country. It has hosted six Super Bowl games.

*Danny Wuerffel won the 1996 Heisman Trophy and started two games for the Saints in '97.*

Copyright © 1997 Michael C. Hebert/Spurlock Photography, Inc.

## INDIVIDUAL RECORDS

### Career

    Rushing Yards:  4,267, George Rogers, 1981–84

    Passing Yards:  21,734, Archie Manning, 1971–82

    Receptions:  532, Eric Martin, 1985–93

    Interceptions:  37, Dave Waymer, 1980–89

    Touchdowns:  53, Dalton Hilliard, 1986–93

    Points:  1,318, Morten Andersen, 1982–94

### Season

    Rushing Yards:  1,674, George Rogers, 1981

    Passing Yards:  3,970, Jim Everett, 1995

    Receptions:  85, Eric Martin, 1988

    Interceptions:  10, Dave Whitsell, 1967

    Touchdowns:  18, Dalton Hilliard, 1989

    Points:  121, Morten Andersen, 1987

## ACROSS

2. Saints' career receiving leader
6. Down and ___
8. Former
9. 1st play of every game
10. Saints' career scoring leader
12. G King or LB Simonini
13. Not visible through Superdome roof
14. Deflect a PAT (init.)
15. Saints' head coach
17. Defeat
20. ___ or die
22. A cheer
23. Head protector
24. Saints' career rushing leader
29. List of players
30. Regulations
32. WR Dwight, G Jeff or DE Mike
33. Former home of the Raiders (init.)
36. Twist
37. Sunday night game network (init.)
39. Toss
41. MNF network
42. Tied team record with 3 TDs in '94 game
44. Willie Broughton's position (init.)
45. Saints' career leader in touchdowns

48. We'll tell you later (init.)
49. Protected by goggles
51. Lead the blocking around end
52. Column heading on roster
54. Leap
56. Point value of a safety
57. Saints' leading rusher in '97
60. The ball is full of it
61. Snapper
62. Top half of a uniform
63. Top player

## DOWN

1. Guard
2. Father of '97 No. 1 college draft pick
3. Type of bread on training table
4. Passes completed divided by passes attempted (abbr.)
5. 1st year player
6. Points ___ turnovers
7. Ducat
9. Leg joint
11. Possible maker of replay screen
16. Run back the opening boot (init.)
17. Brag
18. Part of PAT
19. T-shirt size
21. Run ___ pass?
23. RB
25. Lubricant
26. Threw for team-record 3,970 yards in '95
27. Usual college class of draftees (abbr.)
28. Changes
30. Precipitation
31. Fan
34. Away
35. Publicity (init.)
36. Perspiration
38. Running back in the I-formation (abbr.)
40. C John or WR Lonzell
41. Try (abbr.)
43. Heath
46. Home state of Brady Smith (abbr.)
47. Succession of plays
50. Holler
53. ___-announcer (init.)
55. A division
56. Ball prop
58. CB Bivian, DB Carl or CB Mark
59. Observe

*Solution on page 190*

---

**RETIRED UNIFORM NUMBERS**

Jim Taylor—31

Doug Atkins—81

```
Y  I  T  C  D  W  O  A  N  D  E  R  S  E  N
W  A  K  A  E  K  N  I  R  O  G  L  G  A  E
A  T  R  G  M  B  R  S  J  A  C  K  S  O  N
Y  E  L  G  P  J  R  A  L  A  H  B  N  S  V
M  S  O  B  S  U  A  B  L  E  A  R  U  W  U
E  S  E  O  E  F  R  L  B  C  N  E  E  I  K
R  E  V  Y  Y  E  L  D  E  D  N  A  L  O
G  T  R  S  A  N  R  R  G  U  L  N  E  L  L
N  A  R  T  F  M  A  O  N  P  E  E  V  I  L
I  B  H  A  D  I  A  C  W  K  R  R  I  N  E
N  N  O  I  L  E  V  E  R  E  T  T  R  G  S
N  R  T  L  M  U  N  C  I  E  G  E  D  R  T
A  L  I  G  C  F  U  E  S  M  I  L  L  S  I
M  H  A  O  S  B  S  N  O  S  N  H  O  J  H
S  R  E  G  O  R  M  A  R  T  I  N  P  N  W
```

| ALLEN | GALBREATH | MILLS |
|---|---|---|
| ANDERSEN | GRAY | MUNCIE |
| BATES | HILLIARD | ROAF |
| BRENNER | JACKSON | ROGERS |
| CHANDLER | JOHNSON | ROWE |
| CLARK | MANNING | SWILLING |
| DEMPSEY | MARTIN | WAYMER |
| EVERETT | MAYES | WHITESELL |

# NEW YORK GIANTS

The New York Giants were involved in the first "official" National Football League championship game in 1933. Since then, they have been in 15 other title games, many which were called "the greatest game ever."

The first "greatest game" came before the NFL even decided the champion in postseason play. It was 1927. The Giants were on their way to an 11–1–1 record. The Chicago Bears finished the season at 9–3–2, so when the two teams met near the end of the season in New York's Polo Grounds, the title was still up for grabs. The score was tied at seven when the Bears drove to the Giants' one-yard line, but New York kept Chicago from scoring. Later, the Giants' Hinkey Haines faked a punt from his own end zone and completed a 58-yard pass which set up the winning touchdown. Final score: Giants 13, Bears 7.

The Giants faced the Bears again in the first championship game of 1933, this time in Chicago's Wrigley Field. The lead changed hands six times, but the Bears finally won, 23–21. The Bears' Bronko Nagurski threw a touchdown pass to put Chicago ahead, 16–14, but the Giants scored on a flea-flicker to go ahead 21–16. The Bears bounced back late in the game when Nagurski threw a jump pass to Bill Hewitt, who threw a lateral pass to Bill Karr for the game-winning touchdown.

The Giants got revenge the following year and beat the Bears in the championship game, 30–13. The game was played at the Polo Grounds in nine-degree weather on a sheet of ice. The Giants trailed, 10–3, but New York coach Steve Owen (who guided the Giants for 23 seasons) had his players change from their cleats into sneakers at halftime. The Giants, with improved footing, roared to the win, snapping the Bears' 33-game unbeaten streak.

The Giants lost the championship to the Detroit Lions, 26–7, in 1935, but were going for the title again in 1938. A then-record crowd of 48,120 at the Polo Grounds watched the Giants beat the Green Bay Packers, 23–17. The Giants blocked two first-quarter punts to take an early lead, but it took a 20-yard touchdown pass from Ed Danowski to Hank Soar in the final moments to win. The Packers beat the Giants, 27–0, in a 35-mile-per-hour wind at Milwaukee's State Fair Grounds in the 1939 championship game, then the Bears downed New York, 37–9, in the 1941 title game.

Three years later, the Giants were back in the championship game. Green Bay led, 14–0, but the Giants cut the lead in half on the first play of the fourth quarter. New York threatened the rest of the way, but the Packers hung on for the win.

The Giants lost the title to the Bears, 24–14, in 1946. It was 10 years before the Giants were back in the championship game, but they won when quarterback Charlie Conerly threw for two touchdowns (one to Kyle Rote and another to Frank Gifford), and Alex Webster ran for two scores as New York destroyed the Bears, 47–7.

In 1958, the Giants and Baltimore Colts played the consensus "greatest game ever." With 64,185 fans in Yankee Stadium, the Giants scored first, on a 36-yard field goal by Pat Summerall. The Colts went ahead, 14–3, at the half on touchdowns by Alan Ameche and Raymond Berry. The Giants scored on a one-yard dive by Mel Triplett, following an 86-yard gain on a Conerly-to-Rote pass. New York went ahead, 17–14, on Conerly's 15-yard touchdown pass to Gifford, but the Colts tied it with seven seconds to play on a 20-yard field goal. In the first sudden-death overtime in championship game history, the Colts went 80 yards in 13 plays and won, 23–17, on a one-yard plunge by Ameche.

The same teams played again in the title game the following year. The Giants led, 9–7, going into the final period, but the Colts scored 24 fourth-quarter points to win, 31–16. The Giants lost again in the 1961 championship game when Green Bay's Paul Hornung, who was on leave from his Army duties in Kansas, scored 19 points to lead the Packers to a 37–0 victory. In 1962, the Giants lost to the Packers again, 16–7. And in 1963, New York's third straight championship game, the Giants lost to the Bears, 14–10. Quarterback Y. A. Tittle suffered a knee injury in the first half and hobbled through the rest of the game. The Bears picked off five New York passes.

As frustrating as all those second-place finishes were, the next 20 years were much worse. The Giants struggled for most of the next two decades, and didn't appear in their first Super Bowl until the 1986 season. They made it worth the wait, however, as Phil Simms completed 22-of-25 passes for 268 yards and three touchdowns to earn Most Valuable Player honors as the Giants scored 30 second-half points to beat the Denver Broncos, 39–20.

The Giants were back in the Super Bowl following the 1990 season. New York had the ball for a record 40 minutes, 33 seconds (out of 60 total minutes) and overcame a 12–3 deficit to beat the Buffalo Bills, 20–19. Quarterback Jeff Hostetler, filling in during the playoffs for the injured Simms, hit 20-of-32 passes for 222 yards and a touchdown. Ottis Anderson ran for 102 yards and was the game's MVP. However, the Giants needed for Buffalo's Scott Norwood to miss a 47-yard field goal on the final play of the game to assure their win in the "greatest Super Bowl ever."

*Jessie Armstead has not missed a game in his five pro seasons.*

## INDIVIDUAL RECORDS

### Career

Rushing Yards:  6,897, Rodney Hampton, 1990–97

Passing Yards:  33,462, Phil Simms, 1979–93

Receptions:  395, Joe Morrison, 1959–72

Interceptions:  74, Emlen Tunnell, 1948–58

Touchdowns:  78, Frank Gifford, 1952–60, 1962–64

Points:  646, Pete Gogolak, 1966–74

### Season

Rushing Yards:  1,516, Joe Morris, 1986

Passing Yards:  4,044, Phil Simms, 1984

Receptions:  78, Earnest Gray, 1983

Interceptions:  11, Otto Schnellbacher, 1951, and Jim Patton, 1958

Touchdowns:  21, Joe Morris, 1985

Points:  127, Ali Haji-Sheikh, 1983

## ACROSS

1. Back-up player
5. At
8. Taxi
9. Run
11. Column heading on roster
12. Training table activities
14. Y.A.
15. Giants' career rushing leader
17. Keep your ___ on the ball
18. Giants career scoring leader
20. Place for a nasal strip
23. Column heading on roster
24. Frank and Kathie Lee
25. Ball prop

27. Yards punted minus returns
28. ___ Louis
29. Older player (abbr.)
30. QB was an all-state lacrosse player
32. Title holder
33. Gals
36. No points
38. Halftime entertainment
40. Fellow N.Y. team
42. Wagers
43. Mentor
44. Away
46. Taper
48. Former

50. Do the Giants play in Giants Stadium?
52. Block
54. Past years
55. Month training camp begins
56. Face protectors

## DOWN

1. Texas Southern DE had 14 sacks in '97
2. Running back in I-formation (abbr.)
3. 1st and ___
4. Go ___ guy
5. Stomach muscle (abbr.)
6. Season
7. Protection for broken bone
8. Turns sharply
10. Giants' career passing leader
12. RB/PR was elected captain at two different 4-year colleges
13. Giants' career receiving leader
14. NFL Defensive Player of the Year in '81, '82 and '86

16. Month for mini-camps
19. Iowa G Bob ___
21. Extra session
22. 6-pointers (abbr.)
26. Tied
28. Tastes a drink
30. Game spheres
31. Fire
34. Yell
35. A notion
37. Title hardware
39. Pain
40. Contest
41. Blocking schemes
42. Fan beverage
45. 6–6 and 10–10
47. Danny Kanell's alma mater (init.)
49. Diagrams on play charts
51. ___ Junior (init.)
53. Logo registration (abbr.)

*Solution on page 191*

## RETIRED UNIFORM NUMBERS

Ray Flaherty—1
Mel Hein—7
Phil Simms—11
Y. A. Tittle—14
Al Blozis—32

Joe Morrison—40
Charlie Conerly—42
Ken Strong—50
Lawrence Taylor—56

```
J  Y  U  N  S  T  R  A  H  A  N  O  Y  V  H
E  M  Y  E  I  E  L  D  A  R  A  A  R  A  G
N  N  O  S  I  R  R  O  M  E  W  X  Y  N  O
N  R  B  A  N  K  S  O  P  S  D  N  B  P  G
I  E  I  C  L  S  U  R  T  I  E  A  A  E  O
N  E  S  H  S  L  E  R  O  S  Y  T  V  L  L
G  T  V  I  C  I  E  T  N  F  N  A  A  T  A
S  A  R  O  M  B  R  J  A  I  A  F  R  Y  K
D  U  N  H  O  M  O  R  E  O  K  T  O  G  S
E  R  S  R  X  N  S  H  O  E  L  T  T  I  T
C  O  W  K  E  E  N  U  Y  M  E  E  I  C  B
R  L  R  S  N  D  R  O  F  F  I  G  H  A  R
E  Y  L  A  R  S  F  W  E  D  G  G  Y  I  O
M  A  C  A  R  S  O  N  E  T  A  E  A  G  W
W  T  R  N  N  O  S  N  H  O  J  M  B  R  N
```

| | | |
|---|---|---|
| BANKS | HAYNES | OATES |
| BAVARO | HEIN | ROBERTS |
| BROWN | JENNINGS | SIMMS |
| CARSON | JOHNSON | STRAHAN |
| GIFFORD | JONES | TAYLOR |
| GOGOLAK | MEGGETT | TITTLE |
| GRAY | MORRIS | VAN PELT |
| HAMPTON | MORRISON | WAY |

# NEW YORK JETS

**B**roadway Joe Namath and Super Bowl III. If the New York Jets win the next 10 championships, they still will be remembered most for their stunning upset over the Baltimore Colts at the end of the 1968 season. And Namath, despite an excellent career, will forever be remembered as the man who proved that the American Football League could compete with the National Football League.

The Jets' beginnings, however, were much more humble. The franchise began as the New York "Titans" in the inaugural AFL season of 1960. Sammy Baugh was the club's first coach, and the first player signed was Texas Western College's Don Maynard, who had been playing in Canada. The Titans played in the Polo Grounds and wore blue and gold uniforms. Only 5,727 fans paid to sit in the rain and watch the Titans win their first game over the Buffalo Bills, 27–3. New York finished the season with a record of 7–7, a mark they matched the following season.

Prior to the 1962 season, Baugh was replaced by Clyde Turner. By the middle of the season, owner Harry Wismer was unable to meet the team's payroll and the league office assumed control of the team. On Mar. 28, 1963, a group of New York businessmen, led by Sonny Werblin, purchased the franchise for $1 million. Two weeks later the new owners changed the nickname to "Jets," the colors to green and white, and hired a new coach, Weeb Ewbank. The Jets finished 5–8–1 the following season and averaged just 14,793 fans per home game.

The Jets moved into Shea Stadium in 1964 and recorded their first sellout of 60,300 fans. Rookie Matt Snell ran for 948 yards and was named the AFL Rookie of the Year, but New York finished 5–8–1 again.

A turning point arrived in the ensuing college draft when the Jets used a pick obtained from the Houston Oilers to select Namath out of the University of Alabama. A day after playing in the Orange Bowl, Namath signed with the Jets for a reported $427,000. Namath earned a starting spot by the third game of the season, threw for 2,220 yards and 18 touchdowns and was named the AFL Rookie of the Year. Still, the Jets finished 5–8–1 for the third straight season.

In the summer of 1966 the AFL and NFL agreed to merge in 1970—a decision forced largely by the signing of Namath—and to play a world title game in the meantime. The Jets improved to 6–6–2 that season, but were third in their five-team division. In 1967 Namath became the first quarterback to throw for more than 4,000 yards (4,007), but the Jets improved to only 8–5–1. The Jets were successful at the gate, though, selling out all seven home games.

The Jets started the 1968 season with a 3–2 record, but then won eight of their last nine games to finish 11–3. As the Eastern Division champions, they faced the Oakland Raiders in the AFL title game. Namath threw three touchdown passes, including the six-yard game-winner to Maynard, as the Jets came from behind to win, 27–23.

In the NFL, meanwhile, Baltimore had rolled to a 13–1 record and blitzed the Cleveland Browns, 34–0, in the NFL championship game. The Colts were an 18-point favorite to beat the Jets, but Namath had other ideas.

Namath was a perfect symbol for the free-spirited 1960s. He was long-haired, cocky, rebellious, and an unabashed playboy—the opposite of Baltimore's crew-cut, clean-cut quarterback, Earl Morrall. It was a matchup that perfectly captured the generation gap at the time. Fans tended to fall behind one team or the other according to age, although women of all ages seemed to root for Namath.

Namath was the focus of attention in the days leading up to the game. Before he even got out of the locker room after the win over Oakland, he declared five AFL quarterbacks (including himself) were better than Morrall. In Miami, he egged on Baltimore kicker Lou Michaels at a Ft. Lauderdale night club and nearly started a fight, but later gave Michaels a ride back to his hotel. He slept through a team photo session and was fined $50. He granted a pool-side interview to a few reporters as he opened fan mail from young women. Finally, at a banquet honoring his selection as Player of the Year by the Miami Touchdown Club, he dropped the final bombshell: "We are going to win Sunday," he said. "I guarantee you."

And he made his prediction come true. The Jets intercepted three first-half passes and the New York defense stymied the Colts all day. Namath threw for 206 yards (133 of them to George Sauer) and was voted the game's Most Valuable Player. Snell ran for 121 yards. Namath, ever the swinging bachelor, walked out of the stadium that night accompanied by two policemen with guard dogs and two beautiful women. He was the most popular athlete in the country at the time. He was given movie roles and paid huge sums to endorse products—even women's panty hose.

The Jets haven't come close to matching that season since. They won their division again in 1969, but lost a playoff game to the Kansas City Chiefs, 13–6. The following year, after the two leagues had merged, Namath broke his wrist in a rematch with the Colts and was out for the year. The Jets fell to 4–10. The injury-plagued Namath left the Jets in 1976 to play the last year of his career with the Los Angeles Rams.

The Jets went 11–5 in 1981 and made the playoffs as a Wild Card team, but lost in the first round. They made it all the way to the American Football Conference championship game in the strike-shortened 1982 season, before losing to the Miami Dolphins, 14–0. New York returned to the playoffs as a Wild Card team in 1985 (11–5), '86 (10–6) and '91 (8–8), but it did not advance to the title game.

*Copyright © 1997 Michael C. Hebert/Spurlock Photography, Inc.*

*Keyshawn Johnson has caught 133 passes in his first two seasons.*

## INDIVIDUAL RECORDS

### Career

 Rushing Yards: 8,074, Freeman McNeil, 1981–92

 Passing Yards: 27,057, Joe Namath, 1965–76

 Receptions: 627, Don Maynard, 1960–72

 Interceptions: 34, Bill Baird, 1963–69

 Touchdowns: 88, Don Maynard, 1960–72

 Points: 1,470, Pat Leahy, 1974–91

### Season

 Rushing Yards: 1,331, Freeman McNeil, 1985

 Passing Yards: 4,007, Joe Namath, 1967

 Receptions: 93, Al Toon, 1988

 Interceptions: 12, Dainard Paulson, 1964

 Touchdowns: 14, Art Powell, 1960, Don Maynard, 1965, and
   Emerson Boozer, 1972

 Points: 145, Jim Turner, 1968

## ACROSS

1. QB, HB and FB
7. Beat
10. Golfing great
12. Breakfast food
13. Emerson
14. QB sweep: ___ out
17. Jets' career rushing leader
19. Ball prop
20. Scored a team-record 4 TDs in '86 game
21. ___-announcer (init.)
23. Angry
24. 6-pointers (abbr.)
26. Curley
30. Set team record with 93 catches in '88
32. Go ___ it!
33. Wagers
35. A cheer
37. Booted the ball on 4th down
38. Jets' coach, 1995–96
41. Even
42. Deflect a FGA (init.)
43. Column heading on roster (abbr.)
45. Protection for groin area
47. Expected landing of charter (init.)
49. Passes completed divided by passes attempted (abbr.)

51. Publicity (init.)

52. Jets' leading rusher, 1995–97

54. Player's history

56. Pain

58. Usual vocation of agent

59. Do the Jets play in Giants Stadium?

61. Middle of defensive line (init.)

62. Tossed

63. Weird

64. Help on a tackle

## DOWN

2. Decision by official

3. Opponent

4. TD + Safety

5. Ronnie Dixon's position (init.)

6. Shoulder, hip or knee

8. One-third of a yard

9. Kicked team-record 34 field goals in '68

11. Fans in the stands

13. Jets' career interceptions leader

15. East coast rival (init.)

16. Jets' career scoring leader

17. When he retired in '72, he was the NFL's career receiving leader

18. Predicted a win in Super Bowl III

22. Away

25. Tally

27. Led Jets with 6 interceptions in '95 and '97

28. Before side or after Johns

29. Snapper

31. QB in Super Bowl XXX with Steelers

34. Unit on 4th downs

36. TV talk: ___, Mom!

39. Go ___ guy

40. Highest point

42. Slingin' Sammy

44. Extra session (abbr.)

46. Give pleasure

48. Logo registration (abbr.)

50. Yells

51. Participates

53. Mo

55. Rushed

57. A lineman

60. ___ Louis

*Solution on page 191*

## RETIRED UNIFORM NUMBERS

Joe Namath—12

Don Maynard—13

```
D  M  U  R  R  E  L  L  P  O  K  C  E  L  K
A  A  C  S  U  R  A  O  B  N  E  S  L  O  L
B  U  A  R  F  I  W  L  D  N  R  N  N  B  E
Y  G  S  K  U  E  S  N  I  B  L  I  H  P  A
R  C  T  S  L  D  B  O  H  B  D  G  A  I  H
D  P  E  L  N  O  T  F  I  L  C  G  R  L  Y
H  A  R  D  O  F  F  G  L  R  I  I  O  L  U
E  T  F  R  I  N  G  G  L  W  E  R  U  E  A
L  O  R  A  W  S  A  C  A  A  E  U  G  R  E
L  O  O  N  S  L  H  L  I  Z  H  C  A  S  N
I  N  Z  Y  F  T  K  M  O  O  R  E  E  S  I
E  Z  N  A  A  E  O  O  K  L  L  E  N  S  T
N  O  E  M  R  M  B  O  T  N  Z  E  I  S  S
C  U  A  A  N  O  S  N  H  O  J  N  M  E  A
M  N  B  O  D  O  N  N  E  L  L  O  W  D  G
```

| | | |
|---|---|---|
| BIGGS | KLECKO | PHILBIN |
| BOOZER | LEAHY | PILLERS |
| BYRD | MAYNARD | POWELL |
| CASTER | MCNEIL | RIGGINS |
| CLIFTON | MOORE | SAUER |
| GASTINEAU | MURRELL | SNELL |
| HILL | NAMATH | TOON |
| JOHNSON | O'DONNELL | WALKER |

# OAKLAND RAIDERS

**C**ontrary to popular belief, the Raiders, technically, were not part of the original American Football League. Sure, they played in the AFL's first season, 1960. However, when a meeting was held on Aug. 14, 1959, to form the league, just six cities were represented: Dallas, New York, Houston, Denver, Los Angeles and Minneapolis. Three months later Buffalo and Boston were added. The first draft was held on Nov. 22, 1959, and still no Raiders.

The Raiders became a reality on Jan. 30, 1960. The Minneapolis/St. Paul franchise was struggling to get off the ground and was reassigned to Oakland. Two months later a special draft was conducted to stock the Raiders with players. Eddie Erdelatz was the first head coach.

The Raiders started slowly. They were 6–8 in their first season, then 2–12 in 1961 and 1–13 in '62. Then a fiery, brash, young assistant coach from the San Diego Chargers named Al Davis was brought in. As the receivers coach with the Chargers, Davis had developed the most feared and imitated passing attack in the AFL. However, he never had been a head coach, serving as an assistant with Adelphi College, the Baltimore Colts, The Citadel, the University of Southern California and the Chargers.

Davis immediately introduced an explosive offense and new concepts on defense. The league office also allowed the two last-place teams—the Raiders and New York Titans—to select a handful of players from the other teams in hopes of providing a more competitive balance. The Raiders took advantage and improved to 10–4 in Davis' first season. The improvement was nine wins over the previous season and was the greatest victory swing from one year to the next in professional football history. Davis was named the AFL Coach of the Year.

Two years later the league finally found a way to stop Davis. It named him AFL commissioner. Davis didn't like the job, however, and quit within four months to return to Oakland as the managing general partner. Under coach John Rauch, the Raiders finished 8–5–1.

Prior to the 1967 season, the Raiders acquired quarterback Daryle Lamonica from the University of Notre Dame. He was the league's leading passer that year with 3,227 yards and guided Oakland to a 13–1 record. The Raiders defeated the Houston Oilers, 40–7, in the AFL championship game, then advanced to Super Bowl II against the Green Bay Packers. The Raiders were beaten, 33–14, in Miami. The following year they tied for the division title with a 12–2 record. They beat the Kansas City Chiefs, 41–6, in a playoff, then lost to the New York Jets, 27–23, for the AFL title.

On Feb. 4, 1969, the Raiders began a new era. Rauch left to take a job with the Buffalo Bills and was replaced by Raiders assistant John Madden. Madden remained in that position for 10 seasons.

The Raiders won their division seven times under Madden and finished second the other three years. Still, they were frustrated in postseason play, losing the AFL title game to Kansas City in 1969, losing the American Football Conference title game to Baltimore the following year and losing to the Pittsburgh Steelers in the first round in 1972.

The breakthrough came in 1976. Perennial all-pro center Jim Otto, the last of the original Raiders, had just retired, but Oakland was well stocked with Ken Stabler at quarterback, Mark van Eeghen in the backfield and receivers Cliff Branch and Dave Casper. The Raiders lost just one regular season game—48–17 to the New England Patriots—then beat New England and Pittsburgh in the playoffs to advance to Super Bowl XI. There, they gained a record 429 yards (since broken), led by wide receiver Fred Biletnikoff (the game's Most Valuable Player), and coasted past the Minnesota Vikings, 32–14.

Tom Flores, the club's first quarterback, replaced Madden in 1979. By 1980, Flores had the Raiders back in the Super Bowl where they won again, beating the Philadelphia Eagles, 27–10, in New Orleans. Meanwhile, Davis was trying to move his team to Los Angeles. The league balked, but Davis pursued the matter in court. Finally, prior to the 1982 season, the courts approved the move.

The Raiders continued to win in Los Angeles. They had a league-best 8–1 record in the strike-shortened 1982 season, then won the Super Bowl again in 1983, downing the Washington Redskins, 38–9, as Marcus Allen won MVP honors. Since then, the Raiders have won division titles in 1985 (under Flores) and '90 (under Art Shell), but have not been back to the Super Bowl.

In the summer of 1995, Davis opted to move the Raiders back to Oakland, leaving the L.A. area without an NFL team.

Aside from Davis, the Raiders have featured two of the more intriguing men in NFL history. One was George Blanda, the Hall of Fame quarterback and kicker. Blanda finished his career with the Raiders, playing with them from 1967–75. He was 48 years old when he retired, a veteran of 26 NFL seasons. He became the first player in league history to surpass 2,000 career points in his final season.

The other was Bo Jackson, who excelled in both professional football and baseball. Jackson, originally the first player taken in the draft by the Tampa Bay Buccaneers, chose to play baseball instead. He later took on football as well, signing with the Raiders in 1987. He played just three seasons, but left his mark. He rushed for a team-record 221 yards against the Seattle Seahawks in 1987. He has had three of the four longest runs in team history (92, 91 and 88 yards). And he led the team in rushing in 1989 and '90, averaging better than 5.5 yards per carry. A freak hip injury forced him into early retirement from football, although he had hip replacement surgery and was able to return to the baseball diamond.

*Tim Brown is the only Raider to score on a pass reception, rush, kickoff return and punt return.*

## INDIVIDUAL RECORDS

### Career

Rushing Yards:  8,545, Marcus Allen, 1982–92

Passing Yards:  19,078, Ken Stabler, 1970–79

Receptions:  599, Tim Brown, 1988–97

Interceptions:  39, Willie Brown, 1967–78, and Lester Hayes, 1977–86

Touchdowns:  98, Marcus Allen, 1982–92

Points:  863, George Blanda, 1967–75

### Season

Rushing Yards:  1,759, Marcus Allen, 1985

Passing Yards:  3,917, Jeff George, 1997

Receptions:  104, Tim Brown, 1997

Interceptions:  13, Lester Hayes, 1980

Touchdowns:  18, Marcus Allen, 1984

Points:  132, Jeff Jaeger, 1993

## ACROSS

1. Publicity (init.)
2. A cheer
8. Swap
12. Raiders' career leader in FGs had 162 from 1980–88
13. Game sphere
16. Down and ___
18. Unsigned player (init.)
19. Raiders' career rushing leader
20. One time
22. Possible college major (init.)
23. Protected by a flak jacket
24. A lineman
25. All right
26. 4th down boot
27. Allow
29. Point value of PAT
30. Major penalty: pass ___
32. Raiders' career receiving leader
34. Ump's relative
35. Beside the RG
37. Bills' Simpson
40. Roaming DB
41. Raiders' career scoring leader
43. Remnants of celebratory cigars
46. MNF network
48. Time zone for Baltimore (init.)
49. Point total for Raiders at start of game

50. Force into traffic
52. Palindromic center
55. ___-announcer (init.)
56. Stop play (abbr.)
57. TE set a team record with 12 catches in '76 game
59. Sass
60. Set a team record in 1st season with 3,917 passing yards in '97
62. Deflect a FGA (init.)
63. Mike Morton's position (abbr.)
65. Pat Harlow's position (init.)
67. Set team records with 4 TDs and 247 yards receiving in '63 game
69. Raiders' QB in Super Bowl II
70. Location
72. '82 NFL Coach of the Year
73. Tear
74. Number of Super Bowl wins by the Raiders

## DOWN

1. Paid player
3. Stomach muscle (abbr.)
4. Set a team record with 13 interceptions in '80
5. Pick up a loose ball (init.)
6. Heavy RB
7. Home state of Russell Maryland (abbr.)
9. Runback (abbr.)
10. One who guards
11. Raiders' career passing leader
14. Gone by
15. Holds uniforms and towels
17. Snapper

21. Not any
22. Jeff George's 1st college (init.)
23. Rush
26. Bottom half of a uniform
28. Before defeated or sportsmanlike
29. Points ___ turnovers
30. Down and ___
31. Beside the RT
32. Award for nation's top collegiate receiver is named in his honor
33. Walk through water
36. Muscular contraction
38. Set team record with 132 points in '93
39. Against (abbr.)
40. James Fulston's home state (abbr.)
42. Try (abbr.)
44. Usual college class of draftee (abbr.)
45. Set team record with 424 passing yards in '93 game
47. Raiders' head coach
50. Bo
51. Wide left
53. Before side or after Johns
54. 8-time Pro Bowl T, also coached Raiders for 6 years
58. Baseball stat (init.)
61. ___ to guy
64. Star of the game
66. Reminder of injury
68. TV talk: ___, Mom!
70. Covers the TE
71. Lance Johnstone's position (init.)

*Solution on page 192*

## RETIRED UNIFORM NUMBERS
None

```
A  D  N  A  L  B  B  S  N  O  S  K  C  A  J
N  E  L  L  A  R  A  Y  L  E  N  A  N  N  A
N  L  Y  L  O  J  U  B  L  N  R  V  V  E  R
I  F  D  W  E  G  R  O  E  G  O  C  K  S  R
L  E  N  F  Y  H  R  R  W  S  I  A  N  C
Y  R  E  F  T  B  S  E  O  A  F  H  U  E  L
S  E  R  O  L  F  L  R  P  H  O  V  I  T  A
R  L  I  K  S  E  Y  A  H  S  C  H  T  S  N
E  L  C  I  X  Y  E  R  D  P  A  B  P  I  A
A  C  I  N  O  M  A  L  D  U  R  C  A  R  M
N  Q  U  T  S  R  E  L  T  E  T  S  O  H  F
R  I  T  E  C  L  S  I  V  A  D  R  H  C  U
U  O  C  L  E  N  L  L  O  S  S  D  H  O  A
T  M  V  I  R  S  H  E  R  K  E  C  I  A  K
R  E  L  B  A  T  S  O  W  H  C  N  A  R  B
```

| | | |
|---|---|---|
| ALLEN | DALBY | KAUFMAN |
| BAHR | DAVIS | LAMONICA |
| BILETNIKOFF | FLORES | OTTO |
| BLANDA | GEORGE | POWELL |
| BRANCH | GUY | SHELL |
| BROWN | HAYES | STABLER |
| CASPER | HOSTETLER | UPSHAW |
| CHRISTENSEN | JACKSON | WELLS |

# PHILADELPHIA EAGLES

The first professional football team in the Philadelphia area was the Frankford Yellow Jackets in 1924. They led the league in victories in each of their first three seasons, but won the championship just once (1926) because not all of the teams played the same number of games. That franchise folded midway through the 1931 season.

Two years later, the National Football League offered the franchise to a Philadelphia syndicate headed by Bert Bell and Lud Wray for $2,500. The team was named "Eagles" in honor of the symbol of the New Deal and the National Recovery Administration. After two losing seasons, Bell proposed that the league hold an annual draft of college players, with teams selecting in an inverse order of finish. Prior to then, teams would bid on the better players, driving the price of doing business higher than what the owners could afford. The idea was approved, and in May of 1936 the first NFL draft was conducted. It so happened that Philadelphia had finished the 1935 season in last place (2–9), and had the first pick in the history of the NFL draft. The Eagles selected the first Heisman Trophy winner, halfback Jay Berwanger of the University of Chicago.

Unfortunately for Philadelphia, Berwanger had no desire to play pro football. The Eagles traded his rights to the Chicago Bears, but Berwanger never did play.

The Eagles finally got the player of their choice in 1939 when they signed Texas Christian University all-America quarterback Davey O'Brien for a reported $12,000 a year and a percentage of the gate. In his rookie season O'Brien set an NFL record (since broken) with 1,324 passing yards. That same season the Eagles also were part of television history. They played in the first televised professional football game at Brooklyn's Ebbets Field, losing to the Brooklyn Dodgers, 23–14. Allan "Skip" Walz broadcast the game for NBC to approximately 1,000 households in New York.

In 1940 Art Rooney of Pittsburgh bought half of the Eagles franchise. A year later Rooney and Bell swapped franchises with Pittsburgh's Alexis Thompson, who owned the Pittsburgh Pirates (which became the Steelers). In 1943 those same businessmen shared even more. They decided to consolidate their franchises during the war and became the Philadelphia-Pittsburgh "Steagles." The extra manpower helped. They went 5–4–1, the first time the Eagles finished above .500.

With the war winding down in 1945, the Eagles got most of their players back, along with their draft pick, halfback Steve Van Buren. They improved to 7–1–2 and finished in second place. The next year, Van Buren led the league in rushing (the first of four times), and the Eagles finished second again at 7–3. The Eagles made it three straight second-place finishes in 1946, then tied Pittsburgh for the Eastern Division title the following season with an 8–4 record. The Eagles won the division playoff game over their intra-state rival, 21–0, and advanced to their first championship game. They lost, however, to the Chicago Cardinals, 28–21.

The Eagles were back in the title game the next two years and won back-to-back championships. In 1948 they were 9–2–1 in the regular season, then beat the Cardinals, 7–0, in a blinding snow storm. The following season they were a league-best 11–1, then beat the Los Angeles Rams, 14–0, for the title.

The Eagles didn't return to the championship game until 1960. Quarterback Norm Van Brocklin and center/linebacker Chuck Bednarik (one of the last men to play both offense and defense throughout the game), led the Eagles to a 10–2 mark and their first conference title in 11 years. They came from behind in the title game to beat the Green Bay Packers, 17–13. After the game, Van Brocklin (who was the league's Most Valuable Player) and coach Buck Shaw announced their retirements.

Philadelphia found able replacements, though. Sonny Jurgensen stepped in at quarterback and threw for a record 3,723 yards (since broken). Nick Skorich was named the new coach, and the Eagles finished 10–4. A rash of injuries rocked the Eagles in 1962, however, beginning a long dry spell. They had just one winning season from 1962 until '78.

In 1976 the Eagles hired coach Dick Vermeil from UCLA. In two years, the workaholic Vermeil elevated Philadelphia to a 9–7 record and a spot in the playoffs. Vermeil's Eagles made the playoffs four straight years, and in 1980, led by quarterback Ron Jaworski (the National Football Conference Player of the Year) and wide receiver Harold Carmichael, the Eagles went 12–4 and advanced to Super Bowl XV. They lost to the Oakland Raiders, 27–10.

The Eagles were 3–6 in the strike-shortened 1982 season, and a burned-out Vermeil retired. The Eagles struggled until Buddy Ryan was named coach in 1986. He, along with standout players such as quarterback Randall Cunningham and defensive end Reggie White, led the team to a share of their division title in 1988 and to Wild Card playoff spots in '89 and '90. After the team finished 10–6—but out of the playoffs—in 1991, Ryan was fired.

The Eagles returned to the playoffs in 1992 with an 11–5 record, their fifth straight 10-plus win season. Heath Sherman, a relatively unknown running back, led the NFL with an average of 5.2 yards per carry. The Eagles failed to make postseason play in 1993 and '94, but finished 10–6 in each of the next two seasons to earn a playoff spot. Philadelphia slipped to 6–9–1 in 1997.

*Copyright © 1997 Michael C. Hebert/Spurlock Photography, Inc.*

*In just three seasons, Ricky Watters ranks fourth on the Eagles' career rushing list.*

## INDIVIDUAL RECORDS

### Career

    Rushing Yards:  6,538, Wilbert Montgomery, 1977–84

    Passing Yards:  26,963, Ron Jaworski, 1977–86

    Receptions:  589, Harold Carmichael, 1971–83

    Interceptions:  34, Bill Bradley, 1969–76

    Touchdowns:  79, Harold Carmichael, 1971–83

    Points:  881, Bobby Walston, 1951–62

### Season

    Rushing Yards:  1,512, Wilbert Montgomery, 1979

    Passing Yards:  3,808, Randall Cunningham, 1988

    Receptions:  88, Irving Fryar, 1996

    Interceptions:  11, Bill Bradley, 1971

    Touchdowns:  18, Steve Van Buren, 1945

    Points:  116, Paul McFadden, 1984

## ACROSS

1. Defend with 2 players
7. Plead
9. Force into traffic
11. Yards gained divided by carries
12. Reveals
13. Spins
15. Championship
18. 1st word of the national anthem
20. Coach Khayat or K Murray
22. WR
23. Eagles' career interceptions leader
24. RB has been in George Foreman's corner for several fights
26. ___ Louis
29. Upstart league
30. Go deep!
32. Eagles' career rushing leader
34. Quick snooze
35. Before right or after warm
36. WR is a licensed ordained minister
39. Omit
41. WR
43. Veer to the sideline
45. Twirlers' equipment

46. Eagles' career leader in kickoff and punt returns
49. Linemen
51. Willie T
53. ___ corner kick
55. Pierce
57. Column heading on roster
58. Only Eagle to play 14 seasons
59. Query
61. Leg joint
62. Pick off a pass (abbr.)
63. Point value of PAT

## DOWN

2. Down and ___
3. Hard throws
4. Eagles' division
5. Defeats
6. Penalty: ___ guarding
7. Wager
8. Obtain
9. Sonny
10. Face ___
14. Close to the ground
16. Was ahead
17. Eagles' career passing leader
19. DT was waived 6 times before catching on with 49ers and Eagles
21. '90 Heisman Trophy winner
23. Deflect a FGA (init.)
25. Blocking from behind
27. Richard Cooper's position (init.)
28. Back-up QB is the grandson of 1B Wally Post
30. Quarters in a game
31. Favorite response of movie character Rocky, a Philly native
33. Rival sports league (init.)
36. Screw up
37. Column heading on roster (abbr.)
38. Buddy
40. Post-season games
42. Eagles' career scoring leader
44. Ends, tackles, guards and center
47. Eagles' head coach
48. Rodney Peete's alma mater (init.)
50. Victory
51. Back in I-formation (abbr.)
52. Hike
54. Place for nasal strips
56. Off-season water sport
59. Away
60. 1st play of every game (init.)

*Solution on page 192*

---

**RETIRED UNIFORM NUMBERS**

Steve Van Buren—15

Tom Brookshier—40

Pete Retzlaff—44

Chuck Bednarik—60

Al Wistert—70

Jerome Brown—99

```
B  T  C  U  N  N  I  N  G  H  A  M  N  Y  Y
L  A  C  N  S  N  A  G  O  L  C  C  E  O  G
L  H  L  K  I  R  A  N  D  E  B  D  I  R  N
A  H  A  L  S  T  A  A  L  E  W  O  L  L  L
H  I  R  R  E  S  M  Y  T  A  J  N  O  I  U
I  P  K  P  M  N  A  I  R  L  A  A  L  K  L
H  I  E  A  O  R  H  D  T  F  C  L  E  S  E
I  S  S  R  R  W  S  I  R  U  K  D  N  E  A
K  E  R  B  E  N  E  Y  E  S  S  N  O  R  H
S  A  M  A  E  L  A  S  N  I  O  D  T  O  C
R  R  W  K  Y  R  O  E  A  Y  N  P  S  F  I
O  S  Y  E  Y  B  A  N  W  O  R  B  L  E  M
W  U  A  R  Y  D  T  S  R  E  T  T  A  W  R
A  M  O  N  T  G  O  M  E  R  Y  E  W  A  A
J  A  T  O  W  E  N  E  R  U  B  N  A  V  C
```

| | | |
|---|---|---|
| ALLEN | EDWARDS | MONTGOMERY |
| BAKER | FRYAR | SEARS |
| BEDNARIK | HALL | SISEMORE |
| BROWN | JACKSON | SNEAD |
| BYARS | JAWORSKI | VAN BUREN |
| CARMICHAEL | KILROY | WALSTON |
| CLARKE | LOGAN | WATTERS |
| CUNNINGHAM | MCDONALD | WHITE |

# PITTSBURGH STEELERS

**D**uring a six-year period in the 1970s, the Pittsburgh Steelers won four Super Bowls and were the dominant team in the National Football League. How did they do it?

The answer: a great coach and great players. Coach Chuck Noll and seven of his players were selected to the Pro Football Hall of Fame. Did great players make the Steelers a championship team, or did the championship teams make players worthy of Hall of Fame status? Whatever the answer, two things are certain. The Steelers drafted each of those seven Hall of Fame players, and as a group those players played 100 of their combined 101 years of pro football in Pittsburgh. The Steelers drafted 'em, played 'em, won with 'em and watched 'em retire.

The Steelers' dynasty began with the hiring of the 37-year-old Noll on Jan. 27, 1969. He built through the draft, starting with the defense. In that year's draft, the Steelers used the fourth overall pick to select Joe Greene, a defensive tackle from North Texas State University. In the 10th round they chose defensive end L. C. Greenwood, who would play in six Pro Bowls.

Pittsburgh was just 1–13 in Noll's first season, so the Steelers had the No. 1 pick in the 1970 draft. They selected quarterback Terry Bradshaw of Louisiana Tech University. They also took Southern University defensive back Mel Blount. With the rookie Bradshaw starting, the Steelers improved to 5–9.

The Steelers used their second-round pick the following year on Penn State University linebacker Jack Ham, and improved to 6–8. In the 1972 draft they added Penn State running back Franco Harris with the 13th overall choice in the first round. With Harris starting (and gaining more than 1,000 yards), Pittsburgh won the American Football Conference's Central Division with an 11–3 record the following season. The Steelers beat the Oakland Raiders, 13–7, in the first round of the playoffs, but lost to the undefeated Miami Dolphins, 21–17, in the AFC championship game.

The Steelers added more talent, although no future Hall of Famers, with the 1973 draft. They tied for the division title with a 10–4 record, but lost to Oakland, 33–14, in the first round of the playoffs.

The Steelers struck gold in the 1974 draft, adding four future Pro Bowl performers: wide receiver Lynn Swann (first round), linebacker Jack Lambert (second round), wide receiver John Stallworth (fourth round) and center Mike Webster (fifth round).

So, over the course of six college drafts, the Steelers (with only one pick in the top seven) gained seven future Hall of Famers and three other players who were perennial all-stars.

Not surprisingly, their record reflected their drafting acumen. They finished 10–3–1 in 1974 and beat the Buffalo Bills and Oakland in the playoffs. They went on to win Super Bowl IX in New Orleans, 16–6, over Minnesota, for the franchise's first NFL championship.

With the "Steel Curtain" becoming the league's most feared defense, Pittsburgh repeated the following season. It finished the regular season 12–2 and beat the Baltimore Colts and Oakland to advance to the Super Bowl in Miami. The Steelers won the title over the Dallas Cowboys, 21–17.

The Steelers won their division again in 1976 (10–4) and '77 (9–5), but were upset in the playoffs those years. They added championships the following two seasons, however. In 1978 they were a league-best 14–2 in the regular season and defeated the Cowboys in the Super Bowl, 35–31. In 1979 they were 12–4 and beat the Los Angeles Rams, 31–19, in Super Bowl XIV.

The Steelers would win no more championships, but they remained competitive throughout most of the 1980s. They reached the playoffs in 1982, '83, '84 and '89. Noll retired following the 1991 season after 23 years as the team's head coach. His teams were 209–156–1, and he was the fifth-winningest coach in NFL history.

Thirty-five-year-old Bill Cowher replaced Noll. Pittsburgh won its division with an 11–5 record in 1992, but lost to Buffalo, 24–3, in the second round of the playoffs. The Steelers were back in the playoffs again in 1993 with a 9–7 record, but lost, 27–24, in overtime, to the Kansas City Chiefs in the opening round.

Pittsburgh won its division in each of the last four seasons. The Steelers lost in the AFC championship game in 1994, but advanced to Super Bowl XXX following the '95 season. Pittsburgh was beaten by Dallas, 27–17, in Tempe, Ariz. The Steelers lost in the second round of the playoffs in 1996 and the AFC championship game in '97.

As great as Noll's career record was (.572 winning percentage), Cowher's currently is better (69–38, .645).

The Steelers are the fifth-oldest team among the active squads in the NFL. They began as the Pittsburgh Pirates in 1933 by Arthur J. Rooney. Byron "Whizzer" White, a future Supreme Court justice, was their first big-money player in 1938. The franchise became known as the Steelers after Rooney sold it in 1940. Rooney bought part of the Philadelphia Eagles and then traded the Eagles back for the Steelers, all in a period of a year.

During World War II, the Steelers combined with Philadelphia for one season and became the "Steagles," and later combined with the Chicago Cardinals for a season. The Rooney family continued operation of the team, but the Steelers' first playoff appearance wasn't until Noll's arrival.

*Kordell Stewart set an NFL record for the longest TD run by a QB (80 yards).*

## INDIVIDUAL RECORDS

### Career

Rushing Yards:  11,950, Franco Harris, 1972–83

Passing Yards:  27,989, Terry Bradshaw, 1970–83

Receptions:  537, John Stallworth, 1974–87

Interceptions:  57, Mel Blount, 1970–83

Touchdowns:  100, Franco Harris, 1972–83

Points:  1,343, Gary Anderson, 1982–94

### Season

Rushing Yards:  1,690, Barry Foster, 1992

Passing Yards:  3,724, Terry Bradshaw, 1979

Receptions:  85, Yancey Thigpen, 1995

Interceptions:  11, Mel Blount, 1975

Touchdowns:  15, Louis Lipps, 1985

Points:  141, Norm Johnson, 1995

## ACROSS

1. Strategy: Game ___
4. Turn sharply
7. Team
10. Mitch Lyons' position (init.)
11. Steelers' career rushing leader
12. ___ and 10
14. ___-captain
15. Coach's diagram: XXX and ___
16. Beside the RG
17. RB was the subject of 80 football cards as rookie in '93, the most in history
21. Had team-record 85 catches in '95
22. CB played 8 years in Chicago before signing with Steelers in '97
24. Allen: The future is ___!
27. Before side or after Johns
29. Spectator
30. ___-___ record (init.)
31. LB at UCLA, he became an all-pro safety for Steelers
32. Block
33. Capacity crowd (init.)
34. Players' animals at home
35. Joel Steed's position (init.)
37. Go ___ guy
38. Yell loudly

39. Extending in the same direction
41. Breakfast food
42. Ron Stehouwer's alma mater (init.)
43. Beyond LT
44. Stop play (init.)
45. Wonderful
49. Run back the opening play (init.)
50. Point value of PAT
51. Steelers' career scoring leader
52. Ref's relative
53. Expected time of landing for charter (init.)
54. RB in I-formation
55. Against (abbr.)
56. Free weekend
58. Lateral on a sweep
59. Leg joint
61. ___ vs. Them
62. Guard
64. OL Petersen and QB Marchibroda
65. Throw
66. ___ or under number

## DOWN

1. Part of PAT (abbr.)
2. Remaining
3. Neither rain ___ snow keeps the Steelers from playing
4. One of 34 Across
5. Steelers' stadium
6. Reality
7. Lynn Swann's alma mater (init.)
8. Point value of safety
9. Steelers' career interceptions leader
13. Steelers' career receiving leader
16. HB
18. "Slash"
19. Column heading on roster
20. Set team record with 141 points in '95
23. Points ___ turnovers
25. Tackles, guards and center (init.)
26. Holding, clipping and offsides
27. 1st word of the national anthem
28. Part of MNF
34. Contract
36. Knot
37. Tournament
39. QB runs for his life
40. Shower snapper
46. Mentor
47. Unit without the ball (abbr.)
48. Help on a tackle
49. NBA's N.Y. entry
52. Tom Myslinski's alma mater (init.)
55. Strives for victory
56. Wager
57. A lineman
58. Rod Woodson's alma mater (init.)
60. Qtr.
63. ___ or die

*Solution on page 193*

## RETIRED UNIFORM NUMBERS

None

```
J O H N S O N P M T N U O L B
T R A C J K L R E L T U B R F
S B D O O W N E E R G D A U U
T L T L N A S T L L U D N T Q
E R B F N H S S Q U S V D H U
W R S Y E P B B U H R R E A A
A O D L P E N E A L E W R F K
R W L I T N N W W O O D S O N
T O L L S E W E D Y N R O I I
F O S T E R O O E E E D N C L
I K I N N A W S R R P Y E E L
C C R E N U Q K N B G T U N O
E A R E L O B E T T I S E Y Y
B M A N S F I E L D H S O A D
T B H T R O W L L A T S K L F
```

| | | |
|---|---|---|
| ANDERSON | GREENE | MANSFIELD |
| BETTIS | GREENWOOD | SHELL |
| BLOUNT | HARRIS | STALLWORTH |
| BRADSHAW | JOHNSON | STEWART |
| BROWN | KOLB | SWANN |
| BUTLER | LAYNE | THIGPEN |
| FOSTER | LIPPS | WEBSTER |
| FUQUA | LLOYD | WOODSON |

# SAN DIEGO CHARGERS

**H**ey, this American Football League is really great!

That's what each of the 27,778 fans in the Memorial Coliseum in Los Angeles must have been thinking on Aug. 6, 1969, when the L.A. Chargers played their first preseason game. Chargers running back Paul Lowe got things off to an exciting start when he returned the first kickoff in the first game of the first year of the league 105 yards for a touchdown.

There were 10,000 fewer people in the Coliseum for the regular-season opener, but they also had a lot to cheer about. Led by quarterback Jack Kemp, a future prominent politician, the Chargers scored two fourth-quarter touchdowns to beat the Dallas Texans, 21–20. Still, the fans were unimpressed. By the final home game, the Chargers were drawing fewer than 10,000 fans, although they won the Western Division with a league-best 10–4 record. They lost to the Houston Oilers, 24–16, in the first AFL championship game.

The Chargers, unable to compete with the Rams, left Los Angeles and moved to San Diego before the 1961 season began. They rolled to a league-best 12–2 record, but again lost to the Oilers, 10–3, in the AFL championship game. The Chargers forced 66 turnovers that year, still an all-time single-season record.

The Chargers were decimated by injuries in 1962, but returned to the winner's circle in 1963 with a league-best record of 11–3. Then they destroyed the Boston Patriots, 51–10, in the title game. Running back Keith Lincoln accounted for 349 yards of all-purpose offense in the most lopsided championship game in AFL history.

The Chargers went on to win five division titles in the first six seasons with records of 8–5–1 in 1964 and 9–2–3 in '65. They lost to the Buffalo Bills, 20–7, in the 1964 championship game and to Buffalo again, 23–0, in the '65 title tilt.

San Diego finished with a winning record in each of the four remaining AFL seasons, but never made it back to the championship game. The Chargers were arguably the best team over the 10-year history of the AFL, with a record of 86–48–6, five division titles and one league championship. The stars in that era included wide receiver Lance Alworth, tackle Ron Mix, running backs Lowe and Lincoln, defensive tackle Ernie Ladd, guard Walt Sweeney, quarterback John Hadl, cornerback Chuck Allen and wide receiver Gary Garrison.

The AFL and National Football League merged prior to the 1970 season. In the new alignment, the Chargers were in the American Football Conference's Western

Division with the Denver Broncos, Kansas City Chiefs and Oakland Raiders.

The Chargers struggled in the NFL. They didn't put together a winning season until 1978, their ninth year in the league. They were 1–3 when coach Tommy Prothro resigned, but Don Coryell took over and guided the Chargers to an 8–4 mark the rest of the way to finish 9–7.

Coryell's passing attack was perfect for the team's all-pro quarterback Dan Fouts. Tight end Kellen Winslow was drafted prior to the 1979 season and quickly became Fouts' favorite target. The Chargers roared to the division title in 1979 with a 12–4 record, but lost in the playoffs to Houston, 17–14.

San Diego won its division again in 1980 with an 11–5 record, then beat Buffalo, 20–14, in the playoffs to advance to the AFC title game. There, the Chargers lost to Oakland, 34–27.

The Chargers made it three division titles in a row in 1981, finishing 10–6. They again advanced to the AFC title game after beating the Miami Dolphins, 41–38, on Rolf Benirschke's 27-yard field goal in overtime, but lost to the Cincinnati Bengals, 27–7, in minus-9 degree (minus-59 wind chill) weather.

The Chargers were back in the playoffs in the strike-shortened 1982 season, but then became a pass-happy team that couldn't defend anybody. Fouts was averaging more than 4,000 passing yards a season. Charlie Joiner set the NFL record for career receptions (since broken). Running backs Lionel James and Gary Anderson were catching the ball as often as they were running with it.

The Chargers finished last or tied for last in three of the next four seasons. Midway through the 1986 season, Coryell resigned and was replaced by Al Saunders. In two seasons under Saunders, the Chargers were 8–7 and 6–10. He was fired and replaced by former Chargers quarterback Dan Henning. In 1990 Bobby Beathard, who helped engineer championships at Miami and Washington, was hired as the team's general manager. Beathard fired Henning, whose teams never finished better than 6–10, following the 1991 season and hired former Georgia Tech University coach Bobby Ross.

Ross appeared to be a short-term coach as well after the Chargers opened the 1992 season with four straight losses. However, they won 11 of their final 12 games, including their final seven, to win their division. They beat Kansas City, 17–0, in the first round of the playoffs, but lost to Miami, 31–0, in the second round. In 1993, the Chargers slipped to 8–8 and missed the playoffs.

In 1994, led by Natrone Means' team-record 1,350 yards rushing, Stan Humphries' passing and a solid defense led by linebacker Junior Seau, the Chargers won their division with an 11–5 record. They beat Miami, 22–21, in the divisional playoffs, then downed the Pittsburgh Steelers, 17–13, to win the AFC title. The Chargers were beaten by the San Francisco 49ers, 49–26, at Joe Robbie Stadium at Miami in Super Bowl XXIX.

San Diego slipped to 9–7 in 1995 and were upset in the opening round of the playoffs by the Indianapolis Colts, 35–20. The Chargers missed the playoffs in 1996 with an 8–8 record. Following the season, Ross was replaced on the sidelines by Kevin Gilbride. The change didn't help. The Chargers fell to 4–12 and tied for last place in their division. They ranked last in the league in points allowed (26.6 per game) and second from last in the AFC in points scored (16.6 per game).

Copyright © 1995 Michael C. Hebert/Spurlock Photography, Inc.

*Junior Seau has been voted into seven straight Pro Bowls.*

## INDIVIDUAL RECORDS

### Career

Rushing Yards: 4,963, Paul Lowe, 1960–67

Passing Yards: 43,040, Dan Fouts, 1973–87

Receptions: 586, Charlie Joiner, 1976–86

Interceptions: 42, Gill Byrd, 1983–92

Touchdowns: 83, Lance Alworth, 1962–70

Points: 766, Rolf Benirschke, 1977–86

### Season

Rushing Yards: 1,350, Natrone Means, 1994

Passing Yards: 4,802, Dan Fouts, 1981

Receptions: 90, Tony Martin, 1995

Interceptions: 9, Charlie McNeil, 1961

Touchdowns: 19, Chuck Muncie, 1981

Points: 135, John Carney, 1994

## ACROSS

2. Leslie Duncan's nickname
7. Shoulder, hip or knee
9. Chargers' career rushing leader
10. Snapper
15. Points ___ turnovers
17. Shares hometown of Shreveport with fellow QBs Terry Bradshaw and Joe Ferguson
20. Beside the RG
21. Contest
23. On the back of a jersey (abbr.)
24. Chargers' career interceptions leader
26. Column heading on roster (abbr.)
27. QB plunge
28. K was named Chargers' Man of the Year for his work with local charities
32. Chargers' career receiving leader
34. Threw for team-record 444 yards in games in '80 and '82
37. Expected landing time of charter (init.)
39. ___ of bounds
41. Team physician (abbr.)
42. WR Kitrick, RB Jessie and LB John
44. Down and ___
47. Observe

49. TE caught a team-record 15 passes in '84 game
51. Scrambled to the right
53. Allen: The future is ___!
54. Ripped
57. Where severely injured players are sent (init.)
58. No game
60. T-shirt size
62. ___ or die
64. At
65. Knocks down
66. Stadium ad
68. Helps on a tackle
69. Getting beat

## DOWN

1. Lance
2. Junior
3. WR Bell or C Flanagan
4. Column heading on roster (abbr.)
5. No attempt to return a punt (init.)
6. Away
7. Paid player
8. Unit without the ball (abbr.)
11. Colleges' governing body (init.)
12. Before right or after warm
13. Former foe in Cleveland
14. Texas WR was a 2-time NCAA long jump champ
16. Spectator

18. Led NFL with 14 TD catches in '96
19. Play ___ or trade me!
21. A cheer
22. Natrone
25. Set team record with 217 yards rushing in '88 game
29. Seasons
30. Coach won 72 games from 1978–86
31. Ralph Perretta's alma mater (init.)
33. Chargers' coach, 1992–96
35. Extra session (abbr.)
36. Go ___ guy
38. Players who begin the game
40. Knot
43. Point value of PAT
45. Chargers' 1st head coach
46. Sean Salisbury's alma mater (init.)
48. Self
50. New Mexico RB led Chargers in rushing in '74
52. William Fuller's position (init.)
54. Squads
55. Observe keys
56. Participates
59. Reuben Davis' position (init.)
61. Middle level defender (abbr.)
63. Column heading on roster
67. Beside the RT

*Solution on page 193*

---

**RETIRED UNIFORM NUMBER**

Dan Fouts—14

```
H  D  R  H  W  F  S  R  E  L  D  N  A  H  C
T  Y  H  C  V  I  P  R  V  L  T  S  E  A  U
R  H  U  M  P  H  R  I  E  S  E  A  N  R  E
O  R  I  N  O  S  R  E  K  L  I  W  N  M  N
W  D  L  K  O  M  G  L  D  N  O  E  O  O  V
L  E  O  D  A  W  M  E  O  R  N  R  T  N  E
A  N  W  C  I  E  A  L  B  X  Y  A  G  H  S
S  S  E  G  A  R  R  I  S  O  N  B  N  H  W
A  K  H  N  R  N  B  S  H  B  O  Z  I  C  E
H  H  S  S  I  U  L  R  M  A  Z  C  H  A  E
A  I  A  T  T  I  O  O  R  U  D  A  S  R  N
L  I  R  T  G  I  L  L  M  A  N  L  A  N  E
L  A  S  E  N  L  L  E  Y  R  O  C  W  E  Y
M  P  U  F  O  U  T  S  I  C  O  N  I  Y  U
R  E  N  I  O  J  W  I  N  S  L  O  W  E  C
```

| | | |
|---|---|---|
| ALWORTH | GARRISON | MARTIN |
| BROWN | GILLMAN | MEANS |
| BUTTS | HADL | MUNCIE |
| BYRD | HARMON | SEAU |
| CARNEY | HUMPHRIES | SWEENEY |
| CHANDLER | JOINER | WASHINGTON |
| CORYELL | LOWE | WILKERSON |
| FOUTS | MACEK | WINSLOW |

# SAN FRANCISCO 49ERS

The San Francisco 49ers should think about changing their nickname to the 79ers. That's the year the franchise struck gold by hiring Bill Walsh.

The 49ers, formed after World War II, didn't win their first championship until after Walsh arrived. They won six division titles, three conference championships and three Super Bowls during his 10 seasons as head coach.

Walsh's first season as coach and general manager in 1979 wasn't exactly a sign of things to come, however. Walsh implemented a new passing attack that ranked first in the National Football Conference, but the 49ers still finished a dismal 2–14, the same record as the previous season. There were signs of improvement in 1980. The 49ers won six games and gave a hint of the offensive explosiveness that would follow. Trailing the New Orleans Saints, 35–7, they came back to win in overtime, 38–35. The 28-point comeback was the greatest in National Football League regular-season history.

By then, Joe Montana, a third-round draft choice, was in place as the quarterback and wide receiver Dwight Clark was beginning to make big catches. In 1981 San Francisco opened the season with three rookies in the defensive secondary, but the newcomers matured quickly. The Niners lost two of their first three games, then reeled off 12 wins in the next 13 games. The 13–3 regular-season record was the league's best. In the playoffs, the 49ers beat the New York Giants and the Dallas Cowboys to advance to Super Bowl XVI in Pontiac, Mich., then held off a fourth-quarter rally by the Cincinnati Bengals to win their first title, 26–21. In three years, Walsh had guided the 49ers from last place to Super Bowl champions.

The 49ers were just 3–6 in the strike-interrupted 1982 season, then lost in the National Football Conference title game in '83. They returned to the Super Bowl the next season, following a 15–1 regular season. After defeating the Giants and Chicago Bears, they faced the Miami Dolphins in Super Bowl XIX at Palo Alto, Calif. Montana completed 24-of-35 passes for 331 yards and three touchdowns and was named the Most Valuable Player of the game for the second time in the 49ers' 38–16 victory.

San Francisco went 10–6, 10–5–1 and 13–2 the next three years, but was beaten in the first round of the playoffs each season. The 49ers made it back to the Super Bowl in 1988, after winning four of their last five games to finish 10–6 and beating the Minnesota Vikings and Bears in the playoffs. In Super Bowl XXIII at Miami, the 49ers beat the Bengals, 20–16. Jerry Rice was the game's MVP, catching 11 passes for a Super Bowl-record 215 yards.

Walsh resigned as coach following his third Super Bowl win in 1989, giving way to defensive coordinator George Seifert, but the 49ers didn't miss a beat. They rolled to a 14–2 record and then sailed through the playoffs, beating Minnesota, 41–13, the Los Angeles Rams, 30–3, and the Denver Broncos, 55–10, in the Super Bowl.

After that, San Francisco finished 14–2 in 1990 (losing in the NFC championship game to the Giants), 10–6 in '91 (missing the playoffs) and 14–2 in '92 (losing in the NFC championship game to the Cowboys). Quarterback Steve Young, who got his chance filling in for the injured Montana, was named the league's MVP in 1992. The team avoided a major quarterback controversy by trading Montana to the Kansas City Chiefs during the off-season, leaving Young in charge. In 1993, Young threw for more than 4,000 yards and led the 49ers to a division-winning 10–6 record. The 49ers advanced to the NFC championship game before losing to the Cowboys for the second straight year.

In 1994, Young again was named the NFL's MVP. He led the 49ers to a 13–3 record and a trip to Super Bowl XXIX at Miami. Young completed 24-of-36 passes for 325 yards as the Niners beat the San Diego Chargers, 49–26.

In 1995, with Young out for four games, San Francisco still won its division for the fourth consecutive season. However, the 49ers were beaten in the divisional playoffs by the Green Bay Packers, 27–17. The 49ers tied for the division title in 1996, but were again defeated by Green Bay in the divisional playoffs. Seifert resigned as the head coach after compiling a record of 108–35 in 11 seasons. He was replaced by 41-year-old Steve Mariucci, the former head coach at the University of California.

San Francisco responded to the coaching change tying for the league-best record at 13–3. However, once again, Green Bay put a stop to San Francisco's postseason play, beating the 49ers, 23–10, in the NFC title game.

The 49ers began play in the All-America Football Conference following World War II. They finished 9–3 in their fourth and final season in that conference, losing in the championship game to the Cleveland Browns, 21–7. In 1950, they were one of three AAFC teams to join the NFL.

San Francisco won more often than not in those early years, and tied for the 1957 Western Conference title. In 1961 the 49ers amazed the football world with a two-quarterback offense. Billy Kilmer would operate out of the shotgun formation. If that didn't work well, John Brodie was inserted to run the offense out of the T-formation. The team finished 7–6–1 that season.

The 49ers struggled through most of the 1960s. Dick Nolan was named the head coach in 1968, and by '70 they had won the NFC's Western Division with a 10–3–1 record. Brodie was named the league's MVP that year, defensive back Bruce Taylor was the Rookie of the Year and Nolan was the Coach of the Year.

That was the first of three straight division titles under Nolan, but the 49ers never were able to reach the Super Bowl.

San Francisco fell to 5–9 and last place in 1973. Brodie and Pro Bowl defensive tackle Charlie Krueger both retired at the end of that season. In 1974, the 49ers used five different quarterbacks and went 6–8. After a 5–9 record in 1975, Nolan was gone. The 49ers went through four coaches in the next three years before Walsh was hired prior to the 1979 campaign.

Copyright © 1997 Michael C. Hebert/Spurlock Photography, Inc.

*Steve Young was the NFL MVP in 1992 and '94.*

## INDIVIDUAL RECORDS
### Career

Rushing Yards: 7,344, Joe Perry, 1950–60, 1963

Passing Yards: 35,124, Joe Montana, 1979–92

Receptions: 1,057, Jerry Rice, 1985–97

Interceptions: 51, Ronnie Lott, 1981–90

Touchdowns: 166, Jerry Rice, 1985–97

Points: 1,000, Jerry Rice, 1985–97

### Season

Rushing Yards: 1,502, Roger Craig, 1988

Passing Yards: 4,023, Steve Young, 1993

Receptions: 122, Jerry Rice, 1995

Interceptions: 10, Dave Baker, 1960, and Ronnie Lott, 1986

Touchdowns: 23, Jerry Rice, 1987

Points: 138, Jerry Rice, 1987

## ACROSS

2. Set team record with 194 yards rushing in '76 game

7. Column heading on roster (abbr.)

8. Can perform

9. ___-announcer (init.)

10. Point value of FG

13. 1st overall pick in the USFL draft, also made the cut at AT&T Pebble Beach Pro-Am

15. John Morton's alma mater (init.)

16. Wide left

17. Winningest coach in 49ers history

19. Ray Brown's alma mater (init.)

20. Chris Dalman's alma mater (init.)

21. Upstart football league (init.)

23. Stylish

24. Longtime CBS play-by-play announcer

25. Gary Plummer's position (abbr.)

27. Mr. Parseghian

28. Great-great-great grandson of Brigham Young

29. Pulls the ball away

32. Passes completed divided by passes attempted (abbr.)

34. Asst. Coach George Stewart's alma mater (init.)

35. Deflect a FGA (init.)
36. Go ___ guy
38. Successive plays culminating in points
40. '81 NFL Coach of the Year
42. 6-pointer (abbr.)
45. Strategy
47. Kevin Mitchell's home state (abbr.)
48. All-pro safety led 49ers with 6 interceptions in '97
50. Spikes
52. Month for mini-camps
54. Whirlpool
55. Kevin Gogan's hometown (init.)
58. K Cofer and WR Wilson
59. 49ers' career interceptions leader
61. 1st year player
63. Prohibited by the league from playing
64. Guarder

## DOWN

1. Pregame stretch
2. 49ers' career leader in FG
3. RB Amp, WR Kevin or CB Mark
4. Wire service (init.)
5. 49ers' head coach
6. 1st word of the national anthem
7. Punting yards minus punt returns
10. Ball props
11. Sunken track
12. Heavy running back
14. Mentor
17. Back-up player (abbr.)
18. Regulation
22. Number representing action on field (abbr.)
26. 49ers' career passing leader
29. Tackle the passer
30. Unusual
31. Yellow flagged
33. ___ strap
34. ___ vs. Them
35. Wager
37. Tackles, guards and center (init.)
39. End zone celebration
41. RB was NFL Comeback Player of the Year in '95
43. Occurrence inflicting destruction
44. Roaming DB
46. Took down the ball carrier
47. Throws
49. Opening plays of games (init.)
51. Slips down
53. In 1st place
56. Part of FS
57. Ends, tackles, guards and center
60. 1st and ___
62. Daryl Price's position (init.)

*Solution on page 194*

## RETIRED UNIFORM NUMBERS

John Brodie—12
Joe Perry—34
Jimmy Johnson—37
Hugh McElhenny—39

Charlie Krueger—70
Leo Nomellini—73
Dwight Clark—87

```
T  R  C  M  U  E  D  S  M  A  I  L  L  I  W
A  O  B  C  H  S  C  E  I  S  T  A  L  A  E
B  H  I  I  N  A  H  I  C  R  A  I  G  Z  R
A  D  A  N  E  T  R  F  R  P  Y  N  E  E  S
H  E  I  T  M  T  I  E  E  O  L  M  S  T  C
A  A  C  Y  N  O  N  R  Y  L  O  C  U  T  H
C  U  L  R  U  L  R  T  I  N  R  R  J  I  I
C  E  A  E  I  Y  U  J  N  A  N  B  E  N  N
I  L  R  E  Y  S  E  O  F  E  H  W  H  E  G
P  L  K  O  I  R  S  H  R  D  E  A  P  E  E
M  I  U  V  O  D  R  N  P  E  R  L  N  P  N
N  N  A  J  O  M  S  S  D  T  S  S  F  K  U
G  D  I  O  A  B  R  O  D  I  E  H  O  L  S
O  A  W  Z  E  A  L  N  G  N  M  T  N  T  A
M  O  N  T  A  N  A  K  D  R  A  L  L  I  W
```

| | | |
|---|---|---|
| BRODIE | JOHNSON | TAYLOR |
| CLARK | LOTT | TURNER |
| CRAIG | MCINTYRE | WALSH |
| DAVIS | MONTANA | WERSCHING |
| DEAN | PERRY | WILLARD |
| HALEY | RICE | WILLIAMS |
| HANKS | ROHDE | WOODSON |
| HART | SEIFERT | YOUNG |

# SEATTLE SEAHAWKS

In 1972, the city of Seattle began construction on what was to be the biggest and best stadium in the nation—The Kingdome. The assignment for a small group of business and community leaders was simple: find a professional football team to play in the new facility.

Two years and a lot of work later, the National Football League granted Seattle a franchise. The principal owner was Lloyd W. Nordstrom, of department store fame. However, the franchise wasn't allowed to enter the league until 1976. The nickname "Seahawks" was selected from 20,365 entries and 1,741 different names. In 1975, the Seahawks began accepting season-ticket applications. They received 24,168 the first day and reached their goal of 59,000 less than a month later.

Jack Patera, an assistant coach with the Minnesota Vikings, was named the first head coach. Nordstrom died of a heart attack while vacationing in Mexico on Jan. 20, 1976, but the team went on. The Seahawks selected 39 players in the veteran allocation draft and 25 more players in the college draft. Defensive tackle Steve Niehaus, from the University of Notre Dame, was the first collegian selected. (He played three seasons before being traded to Minnesota for Carl Eller and an eighth-round pick.)

The Seahawks opened their inaugural season with five straight losses before beating the Tampa Bay Buccaneers, 13–10. Seattle finished the season 2–12. The Seahawks improved to 5–9 in their second season, setting a league record for most wins by a second-year expansion team. The offense, led by quarterback Jim Zorn, was among the best in the league. In a 56–17 win over the Buffalo Bills that season, Seattle rolled up 559 yards. The points and yards are still single-game club records.

Improvement continued. The Seahawks went 9–7 in 1978, and Patera was named the NFL Coach of the Year. Wide receiver Steve Largent was selected to the Pro Bowl, the first of seven appearances in the all-star game.

Seattle was 9–7 again in 1979, but then fell to 4–12. Two more losing seasons followed, and midway through the 1982 season Patera and general manager John Thompson were fired. Mike McCormack was named the interim coach. Prior to the 1983 season, Chuck Knox, former head coach of the Los Angeles Rams and Buffalo Bills, was named the head coach.

Knox, with the help of rookie running back Curt Warner, turned around the team's fortunes immediately. The Seahawks won three of their final four games to finish 9–7 and qualified for the playoffs as a Wild Card team. Seattle surprised the Denver Broncos, 31–7, in the first round, then edged the Miami Dolphins, 27–20, to reach the American Football Conference title game. There, the Seahawks lost to the Los Angeles Raiders, 30–14. Knox was the NFL Coach of the Year and Warner, who gained a club-record 1,449 yards (since broken), was a starter in the Pro Bowl.

The Seahawks improved to 12–4 in 1984. With Warner out all but the first game with a knee injury, quarterback Dave Krieg led the offense by passing for a club-record 3,671 yards (since broken). The Seahawks eliminated the defending Super Bowl champion Raiders, 13–7, in the first round of the playoffs, but lost in the second round at Miami, 31–10.

The Seahawks missed the playoffs in 1985 (8–8) and '86 (10–6), but were back in postseason play in '87 with a 9–6 record. They lost in the opening round of the playoffs that year to the Houston Oilers, 23–20, in overtime.

The Seahawks committed what turned out to be a major mistake in the 1987 supplemental draft when they selected linebacker Brian Bosworth, from the University of Oklahoma, one of their most publicized and expensive players ever. Bosworth wound up playing ineffectively in 24 games over three seasons before he retired with a shoulder injury. He's now trying to stay in the spotlight with a career in Hollywood.

Seattle finished 9–7 in 1988, winning its first-ever AFC Western Division title, but lost to the Cincinnati Bengals, 21–13, in the first round of the playoffs. Prior to the 1989 season, Tom Flores, who had led the Raiders to two Super Bowl championships, was named the Seahawks' president and general manager. Seattle slid to 7–9, then went 9–7. That was the Seahawks' last season above .500.

Following the 1991 season (7–9) the Seahawks and Knox agreed to mutually end Knox's nine-year tenure as head coach. His teams went 80–63, with four playoff appearances and one division championship. Flores assumed the head coaching position, and retained his title of club president.

Flores lasted three seasons; his teams compiled a record of 14–34. He was replaced by Dennis Erickson who won two national championships at the University of Miami. The Seahawks finished 8–8, 7–9 and 8–8 in his first three seasons.

One major bright spot in the Seahawks' history is Largent. Not particularly big or fast, Largent retired in 1989 as the NFL's all-team leader in pass receptions (819), yards gained (13,089) and most consecutive games with a reception (177), records since broken.

*Warren Moon has thrown 279 touchdown passes in his 14-year career.*

## INDIVIDUAL RECORDS

### Career

    Rushing Yards:  6,705, Curt Warner, 1983–89

    Passing Yards:  26,132, Dave Krieg, 1980–91

    Receptions:  819, Steve Largent, 1976–89

    Interceptions:  50, Dave Brown, 1976–86

    Touchdowns:  101, Steve Largent, 1976–89

    Points:  810, Norm Johnson, 1982–90

### Season

    Rushing Yards:  1,545, Chris Warren, 1994

    Passing Yards:  3,678, Warren Moon, 1997

    Receptions:  81, Brian Blades, 1994

    Interceptions:  10, John Harris, 1981, and Kenny Easley, 1984

    Touchdowns:  16, Chris Warren, 1995

    Points:  111, Todd Peterson, 1996

## ACROSS

2. Leg joints
5. Former defensive captain was a sax player
9. Tackles, guards and center (abbr.)
11. Lyle Blackwood's alma mater (init.)
12. James Atkins' position (init.)
14. Seahawks' career rushing leader
15. Good fortune
16. Natrone Means to friends
18. Pierces
20. Cover with two players
21. Turn sharply
23. Star of the game
25. Seahawks' 1st head coach
29. Gamble
31. Team physician (abbr.)
32. Column heading on roster (abbr.)
33. Seahawks' head coach
34. Observe
36. Gate fee
37. WR
39. Gets beat
41. Seahawks' career scoring leader
44. Former
45. Away
46. ___ way or the highway!

47. Pick off a pass (abbr.)

48. Muscular

49. Type of x-ray (init.)

50. 6-pointers (abbr.)

51. Before right or after warm

55. Beside the RG

56. Led Seahawks with 8 interceptions in '97

57. 1st sound during answer at press conference

58. Wait in line for the gates to open

60. Pool stick

61. In 1st place

62. Run

63. Remain

64. Go quickly

67. Ache

68. Deflects

## DOWN

1. Allen: The future is ___!

2. Seahawks' stadium

3. Blunder (abbr.)

4. Take-away

5. Regulation

6. Substitutes

7. Formation: ___gun

8. Column heading on roster (abbr.)

10. Seahawks' career receiving leader

13. HBs in I-formations (abbr.)

16. Former network of AFC

17. Carlester Crumpler's position (init.)

19. Caught team-record 81 catches in '94

22. Accept a challenge

24. Seahawks' career interceptions leader

26. Had a team-record 3 interceptions in '84 game

27. Block

28. Deflect a FGA (init.)

30. Down and ___

32. Head protector

35. Aide

36. Go ___ guy

38. Gear

40. Usual college game days

42. Set team record with 10 interceptions in '81

43. DE led Seahawks with 12 sacks in '97

46. Play ___ or trade me!

52. Tally (abbr.)

53. Tote the ball

54. Against (abbr.)

57. OL Gordon Jolley's alma mater (init.)

58. ___ Louis

59. 2 safeties

60. Easy FG: ___ shot

63. Usual college class of draftees (abbr.)

65. OL Bryan Millard's alma mater (init.)

66. HB

*Solution on page 194*

## RETIRED UNIFORM NUMBERS

Fans—12

Steve Largent—80

```
P  N  E  R  R  A  W  B  C  I  N  G  E  J  N
V  O  N  U  I  H  R  O  W  S  E  A  S  O  E
Y  S  R  I  N  O  S  P  M  I  S  A  D  H  T
K  T  N  T  W  I  I  L  R  L  C  I  N  N  U
R  A  M  N  E  E  U  K  E  N  Y  O  S  T
U  N  O  R  K  R  O  Y  O  F  O  A  M  O  T
W  I  L  L  I  A  M  S  O  U  O  N  D  N  S
N  O  S  N  I  B  O  R  N  R  N  E  E  R  G
U  M  E  O  H  H  E  G  Y  D  E  N  N  E  K
R  X  P  O  S  A  L  F  R  T  K  D  I  B  E
W  A  R  N  E  R  Z  N  E  A  S  N  O  Z  V
I  N  I  N  D  R  X  O  N  T  E  Y  O  W  A
N  O  A  N  A  I  C  T  R  R  D  L  B  X  N
U  S  P  I  L  S  F  S  U  N  E  C  R  E  S
H  D  R  S  B  E  Y  N  T  N  E  G  R  A  L
```

| | | |
|---|---|---|
| BLADES | JOHNSON | SIMPSON |
| BOYD | KENNEDY | TURNER |
| BROWN | KNOX | TUTEN |
| EASLEY | KRIEG | WARNER |
| EDMONDS | LARGENT | WARREN |
| EVANS | NASH | WILLIAMS |
| GREEN | PORTER | YOUNG |
| HARRIS | ROBINSON | ZORN |

# ST. LOUIS RAMS

**Y**ou have your wheelers, and you have your dealers. And then there are the St. Louis Rams.

First, the basic facts: The Rams franchise began in 1937 as the Cleveland Rams. They were 1–10 in their first season. They suspended play for a year in 1943 because of World War II and didn't have their first winning record until 1945. A turning point came in 1945 when the Rams drafted UCLA quarterback Bob Waterfield. In his first season, Waterfield was the first unanimous National Football League Most Valuable Player and guided the Rams over the Washington Redskins, 15–14, for the NFL championship. (Waterfield had some success off the field, too; he married popular Hollywood starlet Jane Russell.) Owner Daniel Reeves moved the team to Los Angeles prior to the 1946 season, and the Rams continued to be among the league's elite for the next decade.

The Rams won their first division title on the west coast in 1949. That year rookies Norm Van Brocklin and Elroy Hirsch emerged, but the Rams lost the NFL title game to the Philadelphia Eagles, 14–0, on a rain-soaked field. In 1950, Los Angeles set 22 league records, went 9–3 and tied for the conference title. They downed the Chicago Bears, 24–14, in the playoff game, but the following week against the Cleveland Browns, Lou Groza's late field goal nipped the Rams, 30–28.

The next season, the Rams won their second NFL championship after going 8–4 in the regular season. L.A. gained revenge on the Browns in the title game with a 24–17 win. The winning points came on a 73-yard pass play from Van Brocklin to Tom Fears.

In 1952, the Rams won their final eight games to finish 9–3 and tied for the conference title. They lost to Detroit, 31–21, in a playoff. The Rams were back in the championship game in 1955, but lost to Cleveland, 38–14. Over the next 10 years (with future NFL commissioner Pete Rozelle as their general manager for part of that time), the Rams had only one winning season. Then in 1967, under coach George Allen, the Rams returned to prominence. L.A. was 11–1–2, but lost to the Green Bay Packers, 28–7, in the playoffs.

The Rams won their division again in 1969, and quarterback Roman Gabriel was the NFL's MVP. Beginning in 1973, the Rams won seven straight National Football Conference Western Division titles, but made it to the Super Bowl just once, in 1979, in the Rose Bowl. The Rams led the Pittsburgh Steelers, 19–17, going into the final period, but the Steelers scored two fourth-quarter touchdowns and won, 31–19.

L.A. was in the playoffs six times in a seven-year period (1983–89) under coach John Robinson, but never got back to the Super Bowl. In 1992, the Rams re-hired former head coach Chuck Knox to take over again. Even with quarterback Jim Everett throwing for more than 3,000 yards for the fifth straight year, the Rams were just 6–10. They were 5–11 in 1993 and 4–12 in '94. With crowds dwindling and a new domed stadium ready in St. Louis, the Rams moved to Missouri prior to the 1995 season. The change of location helped— slightly. The Rams went 7–9 in 1995 and 6–10 in '96. Dick Vermeil was lured out of the broadcast booth and back onto the field as the team's 20th head coach following the 1996 season. The Rams fell to 5–11 and last place in the West Division.

And now, the wheeling and dealing: Of the five trades in league history involving the most players, the Rams were part of four.

On June 13, 1952, the Rams traded 11 players to the Dallas Texans for the draft rights to Les Richter. In exchange for the linebacker and kicker, who made the Pro Bowl seven times in his nine years with the Rams, Los Angeles gave the Texans running back Dick Hoerner, defensive back Tom Keane, defensive back George Sims, center Joe Reid, halfback Billy Baggett, tackle Jack Halliday, fullback Dick McKissack, linebacker Vic Vasicek, end Richard Wilkins, center Aubrey Phillips and running back Dave Anderson.

On March 23, 1959, the Rams traded nine players to the Chicago Cardinals for halfback Ollie Matson (who led the Rams in rushing just once in four years in L.A.). They gave up tackle Frank Fuller, defensive end Glenn Holtzman, tackle Ken Panfil, defensive tackle Art Hauser, end John Tracey, fullback Larry Hickman, halfback Don Brown, the Rams' second-round draft choice in 1960 and a player to be delivered during the 1959 training camp.

On Jan. 28, 1971, the Rams were part of a trade involving 15 players, which tied for the largest in league history. The Rams sent linebacker Maxie Baughan, linebacker Jack Pardee, linebacker Myron Pottios, running back Jeff Jordan, guard John Wilbur, defensive tackle Diron Talbert and a fifth-round draft choice in 1971 to Washington for linebacker Marlin McKeever, first- and third-round choices in 1971 and third-, fourth-, fifth-, sixth- and seventh-round choices in 1972.

On Oct. 31, 1987, the Rams were involved in a three-team trade involving 10 players. The Rams sent all-pro running back Eric Dickerson, who had set a single-season rushing record in 1984, to the Indianapolis Colts. The Colts sent the rights to linebacker Cornelius Bennett to the Buffalo Bills. The Colts sent running back Owen Gill, first- and second-round draft choices in 1988 and a second-round choice in '89 to the Rams. The Bills sent the Rams running back Greg Bell, a first-round choice in 1988 and first- and second-round choices in '89.

However, the biggest trade of all in team history was on July 14, 1972, after Robert Irsay bought the team. Irsay dealt the entire franchise to Carroll Rosenbloom in exchange for Rosenbloom's ownership of the Baltimore Colts.

*Copyright © 1997 Jay Crihfield/Spurlock Photography, Inc.*

*Tony Banks was the NFL's only rookie starting quarterback in 1996.*

## INDIVIDUAL RECORDS

### Career

Rushing Yards: 7,245, Eric Dickerson, 1983–87

Passing Yards: 23,758, Jim Everett, 1986–93

Receptions: 593, Henry Ellard, 1983–93

Interceptions: 46, Ed Meador, 1959–70

Touchdowns: 58, Eric Dickerson, 1983–87

Points: 789, Mike Lansford, 1982–90

### Season

Rushing Yards: 2,105, Eric Dickerson, 1984

Passing Yards: 4,310, Jim Everett, 1989

Receptions: 119, Isaac Bruce, 1995

Interceptions: 14, Dick Lane, 1952

Touchdowns: 20, Eric Dickerson, 1983

Points: 130, David Ray, 1973

## ACROSS

1. Set an NFL record with 2,105 rushing yards in '84
7. Upstart league of the '60s (init.)
9. Get in the way
13. And so forth (abbr.)
14. Roman
16. Quick snooze
19. Leap
21. Spike
22. Rams' career scoring leader
25. Targets
27. For ever
28. Pull along
30. Column heading on roster (abbr.)
32. Rams' head coach
36. DE led team in sacks in '97; ranks among top 10 in NFL history
37. Cease
39. MNF network
42. Away
43. 23-years-___
44. Elroy Hirsch's nickname
45. Pat Haden's alma mater (init.)
46. Publicity (init.)
47. Spin
49. Nebraska RB was 6th overall pick in '96 draft
53. Whirlpool
54. Ball's spin

55. 6-pointers (abbr.)

56. ___-captain

58. Point value of PAT

59. Led Rams with 9 interceptions in '97

61. Exhibition games: ___-season

62. Aide

## DOWN

1. Blitz: red___

2. Rams' career passing leader

3. Covers the TE

4. Column heading on roster

5. Trod

6. Turns sharply

7. Dined

8. Holds players' uniforms

10. QB attended the same HS as Ted Williams

11. Set team record with 5 FGs in '51 game

12. Tackles, guards and center (init.)

15. Rams' career receiving leader

17. East coast foe (init.)

18. Had team-record 119 catches in '95

20. 3rd Super Bowl

23. Dick Lane's nickname

24. Go ___ it!

25. Throwing limb

26. Type of x-ray (init.)

27. OL's cry just prior to a sack

29. Participates

31. Stop play (init.)

33. Beside the RG

34. Former

35. Passes backwards

38. Toy candy dispenser

40. Slides

41. Column heading on roster

45. Before defeated or sportsmanlike

48. Over or ___ number

49. Rams' '97 No. 1 draft pick

50. Offensive, defensive and side

51. Rotates

52. Attempt

53. Tackle the passer

57. Lubricate

60. Before sides or after Johns

*Solution on page 195*

---

**RETIRED UNIFORM NUMBERS**

Bob Waterfield—7

Merlin Olsen—74

Jackie Slater—78

```
E  V  W  N  E  D  L  E  I  F  R  E  T  A  W
C  M  N  N  P  A  R  B  A  S  S  N  S  E  I
U  S  K  N  A  B  N  S  R  T  B  L  I  V  N
R  E  J  B  R  W  N  E  U  R  A  O  N  E  F
B  D  I  E  T  E  O  R  U  T  O  V  S  R  O
G  A  B  R  I  E  L  C  E  P  R  L  T  N  R
H  T  E  S  W  H  E  R  T  E  O  M  E  O  C
N  T  Y  O  U  N  G  B  L  O  O  D  U  S  E
R  E  Y  S  N  L  R  Y  L  E  A  O  M  R  A
E  R  U  R  N  A  T  A  L  H  T  I  V  E  H
H  E  U  A  T  O  N  I  Y  L  T  U  O  D  S
T  V  A  E  A  E  W  P  B  H  E  L  R  N  H
U  E  L  F  N  I  L  K  C  O  R  B  N  A  V
D  I  C  K  E  R  S  O  N  H  I  R  S  C  H
S  E  L  L  A  R  D  E  K  C  I  R  C  J  L
```

| | | |
|---|---|---|
| ANDERSON | ELLARD | RAY |
| BANKS | EVERETT | SLATER |
| BASS | FEARS | SMITH |
| BELL | GABRIEL | SNOW |
| BRUCE | HADEN | TYLER |
| BRUCE | HIRSCH | VAN BROCKLIN |
| COWAN | LANE | WATERFIELD |
| DICKERSON | OLSEN | YOUNGBLOOD |

# TAMPA BAY BUCCANEERS

Tampa Bay was awarded the 27th National Football League franchise on Apr. 24, 1974. Six months later, however, the franchise was in doubt when Philadelphia construction mogul Tom McCloskey backed away from owning the team. Five weeks later, Hugh Culverhouse, a Jacksonville attorney and real estate investor, was awarded ownership.

On Halloween, 1975, John McKay was "tricked" into leaving the University of Southern California, where he had won four national championships, and "treated" with the Buccaneers' head coaching job. The Bucs chose 39 players in the expansion draft the following spring, then used the No. 1 pick in the college draft to select Lee Roy Selmon, a defensive end from the University of Oklahoma. It turned out to be a wise choice.

Tampa Bay opened its inaugural season on Sept. 12, 1976, at Houston, with a 20–0 loss to the Oilers. The Buccaneers were shut out again the following week by the San Diego Chargers, 23–0. Tampa Bay finally scored in Week 3, but it failed to win a game all season. And the Bucs failed to score in five of their 14 games.

Tampa Bay lost its first 12 games the following season, six of them by shutouts. Suddenly, in Week 13, the Bucs came alive and beat the New Orleans Saints, 33–14. Still on a high the following week, Tampa Bay won again, beating the St. Louis Cardinals, 17–7.

Gradually, the Bucs improved by adding high draft picks. USC running back Ricky Bell, the No. 1 overall pick in the draft, was added in 1977. Grambling State University quarterback Doug Williams followed the next year. Lee Roy Selmon, joined by his brother, Dewey, was anchoring an improving defense. The Bucs finished 5–11 in 1978, then stunned the NFL by opening the following season with five straight wins. They finished the season 10–6, winning the National Football Conference's Central Division in just their fourth season of competition.

The city got even more excited when the Bucs beat the Philadelphia Eagles, 24–17, in the playoffs. They then lost to the Los Angeles Rams in the NFC championship game, 9–0.

The Bucs slipped to 5–10–1 in 1980, then won their division again in '81. Their season came down to a winner-take-all final game of the season in Detroit against the Lions. The winner advanced to the playoffs; the loser was home for the Christmas holidays. The Bucs won, 20–17, but were eliminated in the first round of the playoffs by the Dallas Cowboys, 38–0.

The Bucs won five of their last six games and clinched a playoff spot in the final game of the season again the following year in the strike-shortened season. A 26–23 overtime victory over the Chicago Bears propelled them into the playoffs, but they lost in the first round to the Cowboys, 30–17.

Injuries hit the Bucs in 1983 as they lost their first nine games and finished 2–14. They improved only slightly the following year (finishing 6–10) and McKay announced his retirement before the end of the season. The Bucs won his final game, over the New York Jets, 41–21.

Leeman Bennett replaced McKay in 1985 and Tampa Bay had back-to-back 2–14 seasons. A major blow came in the 1986 college draft, when the Bucs gambled and selected Heisman Trophy-winning running back Bo Jackson out of Auburn University with the No. 1 overall pick. The only problem was that Jackson opted to play baseball instead. By the time Jackson was ready to play professional football, the Bucs had lost his rights. He signed instead with the Los Angeles Raiders.

Ray Perkins took over as head coach for the 1987 season. The Bucs drafted quarterback Vinny Testaverde, from the University of Miami, with the No. 1 pick and brought him along slowly. The decision who to start became more complicated when veteran Steve DeBerg threw for five touchdowns in a 48–10 win over the Atlanta Falcons, but Testaverde was back in the starting lineup on Dec. 6 in New Orleans. He quieted the complaints by completing 22-of-47 passes for 369 yards and two touchdowns.

Testaverde continued to throw for big yards, but the Bucs' record did not improve. They were 4–11 in 1987, 5–11 in '88, 5–11 in '89 and 6–10 in '90. With three games remaining in the 1990 season, Perkins was replaced by assistant coach Richard Williamson. A complete house-cleaning took place at the end of the season. Gay Culverhouse was named the new president, Phil Krueger the new general manager and Williamson the full-time head coach.

The appointment didn't last long. Williamson lasted just one season, in which the Bucs finished 3–13. After a complicated courtship of former New York Giants coach Bill Parcells—he turned down the offer to be the team's head coach, then said he would take it, but then was rejected by the Bucs—former Cincinnati Bengals coach Sam Wyche was brought in. Tampa Bay finished 5–11 in Wyche's first campaign in 1992. Testaverde signed with the Cleveland Browns as a free agent after the season, putting second-year quarterback Craig Erickson into the starting spot for most the 1993 season. He threw for 3,054 yards, but the Bucs wound up 5–11 again.

Tampa Bay improved slightly to 6–10 in 1994 and 7–9 in '95. However, Wyche was out, and former NFL defensive back Tony Dungy was in. The Bucs slid to 6–10 in Dungy's debut season, but started strong the following year. Tampa Bay began the 1997 season 5–0, wound up 10–6, and had a winning record for the first time since the strike-shortened '82 season. In addition, the Bucs qualified for the playoffs. In the opening round, Tampa Bay beat Detroit, 20–10; the Bucs lost to Green Bay, 21–7, in the second round.

The Buccaneers were led by running backs Warrick Dunn (978 yards) and Mike Alstott (665 yards), quarterback Trent Dilfer (2,555 yards and 21 touchdowns), and a defense anchored by tackle Warren Sapp (10.5 quarterback sacks), end Chidi Ahanotu (10 sacks) and cornerback Donnie Abraham (5 interceptions).

*Copyright © 1997 Jay Cribfield/Spurlock Photography, Inc.*

*Trent Dilfer was the sixth overall pick in the 1994 draft.*

## INDIVIDUAL RECORDS

### Career

        Rushing Yards: 5,957, James Wilder, 1981–89

        Passing Yards: 14,820, Vinny Testaverde, 1987–92

        Receptions: 430, James Wilder, 1981–89

        Interceptions: 29, Cedric Brown, 1977–84

        Touchdowns: 46, James Wilder, 1981–89

        Points: 416, Donald Igwebuike, 1985–89

### Season

        Rushing Yards: 1,544, James Wilder, 1984

        Passing Yards: 3,563, Doug Williams, 1981

        Receptions: 86, Mark Carrier, 1989

        Interceptions: 9, Cedric Brown, 1981

        Touchdowns: 13, James Wilder, 1984

        Points: 99, Donald Igwebuike, 1989

## ACROSS

1. Campus in Tampa (init.)
3. Toss
8. Martin Mayhew's alma mater (init.)
12. Off the field of play (init.)
13. Championship
15. TV talk: ___, Mom!
16. Symbol of title
18. Wire service (init.)
20. Bucs' career rushing leader
21. Buccaneers, 49ers or Oilers
24. Passes completed divided by passes attempted (abbr.)
25. Team
26. Wear down
27. ___-___ record (init.)
28. Alvin Maxson's alma mater (init.)
29. Mr. Parseghian
30. Nebraska QB Jeff ___
31. Against (abbr.)
32. Only QB to start every game in back-to-back seasons
33. Dine
35. Set club record with 4 TDs in '85 game
36. Bucs' career interceptions leader
37. Down and ___
39. Rival sports league (init.)

41. Water sport
43. Bucs' career leader in receiving yards
46. Tony Dungy's alma mater (init.)
48. Ricky Bell's alma mater (init.)
50. Won '97 NFL Lineman Challenge
52. Bucs' winningest coach
54. Next to the RG
56. On the back of a uniform (abbr.)
57. Seat padding
58. Away
61. Column heading on roster (abbr.)
62. Screams
64. In '96 became 1st Buc to score 3 TDs rushing and 3 receiving in same season
65. Shake his head
67. Middle of defensive line (abbr.)
68. Out of bounds marker

## DOWN

2. Slide
4. Bucs' stadium sponsor
5. HB
6. Column heading on roster (abbr.)
7. Alignment prior to snap
9. Angled pass pattern
10. Stop play
11. Bucs' career scoring leader
14. And so forth (abbr.)
17. Bucs' career passing leader
19. ___-announcer (init.)
22. Win ___ all!
23. Possible maker of replay screen
24. Exhibition: ___-season game
27. Threw for team-record 3,563 yards in '81
28. Skein
30. Give up
32. Bucs' leading receiver in '97
34. Go ___ guy
38. Attempt
40. LaCurtis Jones' alma mater (init.)
41. Taste a drink
42. On the back of a jersey
44. Chidi
45. Running
47. Capacity crowd (init.)
49. Stadium spectators
51. At
53. Dave Alstott's alma mater (init.)
55. Cable network for Sunday night games (init.)
56. The League (init.)
57. Turns sharply
59. Reveal
60. Go deep
63. Observe
66. 6-pointer (abbr.)

*Solution on page 195*

## RETIRED UNIFORM NUMBER

Lee Roy Selmon—63

```
S   C   E   S   R   U   O   D   D   N   O   S   L   I   W
Y   O   T   O   E   R   U   A   U   R   I   C   R   A   R
A   B   T   N   O   M   L   E   S   N   B   A   A   I   O
J   B   E   M   O   S   R   G   M   R   N   N   L   R   R
D   L   H   R   A   P   R   D   A   G   V   N   E   W   E
E   K   R   P   D   I   I   N   I   E   A   O   H   W   B
D   N   P   Y   M   T   T   L   L   E   R   N   O   Y   U
R   W   V   E   Y   L   E   Y   L   E   T   O   U   E   R
E   O   S   L   E   S   E   N   I   Y   D   P   S   R   G
V   R   H   Y   R   N   S   R   W   H   E   T   E   B   G
A   B   A   I   T   T   R   A   I   N   T   T   O   O   R
T   D   M   O   Y   A   T   L   G   E   S   A   R   D   E
S   C   C   K   C   I   L   L   E   B   U   E   O   E   B
E   D   I   L   F   E   R   D   E   N   H   D   L   O   E
T   B   R   Y   O   K   W   I   L   D   E   R   I   A   D
```

| | | |
|---|---|---|
| BELL | DILFER | RHETT |
| BRANTLEY | DUNN | SAPP |
| BROWN | GILES | SELMON |
| CANNON | GRIMES | TESTAVERDE |
| CARRIER | GRUBER | WILDER |
| COBB | HILL | WILLIAMS |
| COTNEY | HOUSE | WILSON |
| DEBERG | HUSTED | WOOD |

# TENNESSEE OILERS

Oil in Tennessee? Just another example of a franchise that hasn't won the most championships or had a lot of star players, but continues to be one of the most interesting clubs in the National Football League.

The Oilers relocated from Houston to Nashville, Tenn., prior to the 1997 season. But wait. The Oilers decided to play in Memphis for two years while waiting for a new stadium to be built in downtown Nashville. Little did the Oilers management know that the citizens of Memphis weren't as thrilled with the NFL as the citizens of the Country Music capital. The Oilers drew more than 32,000 fans for just one home game and played in front of only 17,000 for a pair of games. The Oilers responded with an 8–8 record (6–2 at home), missing the playoffs by just one game.

The Oilers always have been exciting. Consider one year, 1961. It began on New Year's Day when the Houston Oilers won the American Football League championship game following the 1960 season. Rookie running back Billy Cannon (the game's Most Valuable Player) went 88 yards on a pass play in the final quarter to assure a 24–16 Oilers win over the Los Angeles Chargers. Quarterback George Blanda completed 16-of-32 passes for 301 yards and three touchdowns.

Later that fall, the Oilers opened the 1961 season with a rout of the Oakland Raiders in the Bay area while Hurricane Carla was pounding the coast of California. The Oilers proceeded to lose three and tie one of their next four games, and coach Lou Rymkus was replaced by Wally Lemm. The new coach put Blanda on the bench at the start of the next game, but brought him in to throw three touchdowns and kick a 53-yard field goal as the Oilers beat the Dallas Texans, 38–7. The following week, Blanda set an AFL record with 464 passing yards as the Oilers beat the Buffalo Bills, 28–16. Three weeks later, receiver Charles Hennigan caught 10 passes for 214 yards and three touchdowns while Blanda threw for 351 yards and four touchdowns. Blanda also kicked an AFL-record 55-yard field goal as the Oilers beat the previously undefeated San Diego Chargers, 33–13.

The following week, Cannon scored five touchdowns on 373 yards of offense (216 yards rushing, 115 yards in pass receiving and 42 yards in returns) as the Oilers beat the New York Jets, 48–21, in the Polo Grounds. On Dec. 17, the Oilers (despite their 1–3–1 start) won their second consecutive Eastern Division crown by beating Oakland, 47–16. The Oilers were the first professional team in history to score more than 500 points in a season with 513 in 14 games (36.6 a contest). In the week leading up to the AFL championship game, Lemm was named the AFL Coach of the Year, and Blanda was the league's Player of the Year. In the title game on Christmas Eve, the Oilers won their second straight AFL championship with a 10–3 win over San Diego.

The Oilers were one of the original teams in the AFL and didn't waste any time finding players. They signed Cannon, the 1959 Heisman Trophy winner from Louisiana State University, but not until the courts ruled they could. They also signed Blanda, one of the top players in the National Football League. The Oilers went 10–4 in 1960 and won the championship. The excitement continued into 1961 and beyond. Following his miraculous season of 1961, Lemm quit as coach prior to the '62 season to take a job with the St. Louis Cardinals. The Oilers began 1962 by playing the first pro game in famed Harvard Stadium, against the Boston Patriots. Houston went on to win its third straight division title, but lost to Dallas, 20–17, in a historic championship game that took six quarters to decide.

In 1964, Hennigan caught 101 passes in the 14-game season, a pro record (since broken). In 1966, Lemm returned as coach. In his first game back, the Oilers held the Denver Broncos without a first down the entire game on their way to a 45–7 win. Despite that auspicious start, the Oilers finished 3–11.

The next year, however, the Oilers became the first team to go from last place to first in one season, even though they had 15 rookies on the roster. In 1969, the Oilers were 5–6–2 going into the final game, yet still had a chance to make the playoffs—and did. In 1970, linebacker George Webster (the No. 1 pick in 1967) was named to the all-time AFL team, although he played just three seasons in the league. In 1971, safety Ken Houston intercepted two consecutive John Hadl passes and returned both of them for touchdowns.

In 1974, Houston tackle John Matuszak tried to jump to the World Football League, and the Oilers issued a restraining order to him on the sidelines of his WFL game. Two months later, the case was dropped when the Oilers traded him. In 1978, Earl Campbell, a future Hall of Famer, led the NFL in rushing in his rookie season. The Oilers made the playoffs that year and despite losing to the Pittsburgh Steelers, 34–5, more than 50,000 fans greeted the team upon its return to Houston. The Oilers returned to postseason play the following season. Vernon Perry intercepted a record four passes in one game, but the Oilers later lost to Pittsburgh in the American Football Conference title game.

The 1980s were somewhat tame, but the wildest story occurred in the 1992 playoffs. The Oilers led Buffalo early in the third quarter of their first-round game, 35–3. A trip to the second round seemed assured. However, Buffalo mounted the greatest comeback in NFL history and won in overtime, 41–38.

It was just one more in a long line of crazy happenings in Oilers' history. And don't forget about coaches like Bum Phillips, whose unique sense of humor won over fans everywhere, and Jerry Glanville, who left tickets for dead entertainers such as James Dean and Elvis Presley. When you are a fan of the Oilers, the stories never stop.

*Copyright © 1997 Brian Spurlock/Spurlock Photography, Inc.*

*Eddie George was the 1996 NFL Rookie of the Year.*

## INDIVIDUAL RECORDS

### Career

Rushing Yards:  8,574, Earl Campbell, 1978–84

Passing Yards:  33,685, Warren Moon, 1984–93

Receptions:  542, Ernest Givins, 1986–94

Interceptions:  45, Jim Norton, 1960–68

Touchdowns:  73, Earl Campbell, 1978–84

Points:  596, George Blanda, 1960–66

### Season

Rushing Yards:  1,934, Earl Campbell, 1980

Passing Yards:  4,690, Warren Moon, 1991

Receptions:  101, Charlie Hennigan, 1964

Interceptions:  12, Fred Glick, 1963, and Mike Reinfeldt, 1979

Touchdowns:  19, Earl Campbell, 1979

Points:  131, Al Del Greco, 1996

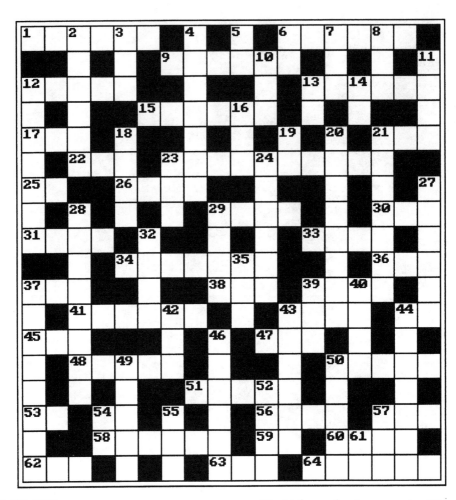

## ACROSS

1. Pulls ball away
6. Sprained ankle or twisted knee
9. Oilers' career interceptions leader
12. 4th down boots
13. An official
15. Ran for a team-record 216 yards in '61 game
17. Column heading on roster
21. Victory
22. Rushed
23. Oilers' career punting leader
25. Brad Hopkins' position (init.)
26. Mild expletive

29. Make a play to prevent a TD
30. Block
31. Yellow hanky
33. Monetary penalty
34. Oilers' prior home
36. Fire
37. ___ Warner League
38. Morse's help
39. Huge blocker
41. Oilers' career scoring leader
43. Tackles, guards and center
44. James Roberson's position (init.)
45. Treatment for sprained ankle
47. Part of foot that kicks the ball

48. CB had a twin brother who played college baseball
50. Push back into the pile
51. Hit
53. 9th Super Bowl
54. Beside the RG
56. Star of the game
57. Pick off a pass (abbr.)
58. 4th Heisman Trophy winner drafted by Oilers
59. List for hurt players
60. Rushes
62. Usual game day (abbr.)
63. Triceps exercise
64. Flattened

## DOWN

2. Ball carrier
3. Kept on the scoreboard (abbr.)
4. Billy "White Shoes"
5. Mike Halapin's position (init.)
6. Down and ___
7. Chuck a TE
8. Baseball stat (init.)
10. Possess
11. Nasty
12. Post-season
13. Before right or after warm
14. Publicity (init.)
16. After time or before side
18. Split and tight
19. A cheer
20. Caught team-record 101 passes in '64
21. Only 4th TE to lead Oilers in receptions
23. Type of x-ray (init.)
24. Oilers' career receiving leader
27. Position prior to snap
28. The Tyler Rose
29. Rests on the bench
32. Oilers' career passing leader
35. Diagram figures: XXX and ___
37. Bum
39. Knot
40. Right after this one
42. CB and S
43. Holds a uniform
44. Unit without the ball
46. Led a sweep
49. Time out beverage
50. Tally
52. Easy FG: ___ shot
54. Next to the RT
55. Attempt
57. Sign a pact
61. CB Mike Davis' alma mater (init.)

*Solution on page 196*

## RETIRED UNIFORM NUMBERS

Earl Campbell—34

Jim Norton—43

Mike Munchak—63

Elvin Bethea—65

```
H  S  J  Y  R  E  M  O  G  T  N  O  M  G  E
S  S  O  H  K  P  P  O  H  S  I  B  I  E  B
P  W  H  H  O  A  L  E  W  I  S  V  I  O  R
G  E  N  L  O  S  C  N  R  E  I  Z  O  R  E
C  H  S  K  H  T  H  T  R  N  A  V  K  G  T
T  T  O  P  G  O  N  E  S  M  U  R  D  E  L
X  T  N  L  U  R  F  E  R  E  L  B  A  T  S
N  A  I  A  O  I  J  E  F  F  I  R  E  S  H
A  M  C  Y  R  N  L  K  K  N  O  R  T  O  N
G  S  A  M  R  I  R  M  A  L  C  A  C  N  B
I  N  O  F  U  H  I  L  L  H  A  U  O  T  E
N  O  I  F  B  L  A  N  D  A  C  N  L  C  T
N  E  T  I  H  W  N  L  E  W  N  N  D  P  H
E  S  D  N  V  K  C  E  R  A  L  A  U  H  E
H  L  L  E  B  P  M  A  C  J  S  A  X  M  A
```

| | | |
|---|---|---|
| BETHEA | GIVINS | MONTGOMERY |
| BISHOP | HENNIGAN | MOON |
| BLANDA | HILL | MUNCHAK |
| BURROUGH | JEFFIRES | NORTON |
| CAMPBELL | JOHNSON | PASTORINI |
| CANNON | LEWIS | ROZIER |
| CULP | MATTHEWS | STABLER |
| GEORGE | MCNAIR | WHITE |

# WASHINGTON REDSKINS

**D**o you want statistical oddities? Then strike up the band and listen to these:

Speaking of bands, the Redskins were the first franchise to have a team band. It began in 1937 and never has missed a home game.

The franchise was founded in 1932 as the Boston Braves, and it played at Braves Field. The nickname was changed to "Redskins" the following year when the team moved its home games to Fenway Park. Then in 1937, the franchise moved to Washington, D.C. In their first season in Washington, the Redskins won the National Football League championship, finishing the regular season 8–3 and beating the Chicago Bears, 28–21, in the title game.

By 1939 the Redskins were finding their place in the records book. That year Frank Filchock, standing deep in his own end zone in kick formation, flipped a pass to Andy Farkas, who ran 99 yards for a touchdown. It is still the longest pass play in NFL history. And in the 1940 NFL championship game, the Redskins had more first downs than Chicago, but still lost. The score? A championship game record: Chicago 73, Washington 0.

In 1942 the Redskins held the New York Giants without a first down and allowed just one yard rushing and one pass completion for the game—but lost. The lone pass completion went for a touchdown, and the Giants scored another touchdown on an interception return on their way to a 14–7 victory. That was the Redskins' only loss of the season. In the championship game that year against the Bears, the Redskins came from behind to win, 14–6.

The same two teams were in the championship game in 1943. Redskins quarterback Sammy Baugh suffered a concussion early in the game while trying to make a tackle and Washington, with a backup quarterback, lost, 41–21.

In 1945 the Redskins lost the title to the Cleveland Rams under freakier conditions. The Redskins were leading, 14–6, but were charged with a safety when Baugh's pass from the end zone struck the goal post (the rule was changed soon after that). Then, following a Rams touchdown, Cleveland's extra point kick hit the crossbar, but bounced through for the winning point.

The Redskins set another record in 1955 when they scored 21 points in 137 seconds against the Philadelphia Eagles. After scoring a routine touchdown and point-after, they recovered a fumble on the Philadelphia 32-yard line. Two plays later the Redskins scored on a pass play. Philadelphia fumbled again on its next possession, Washington recovered on the 13-yard line, scored again and won the game, 31–30.

The Redskins unveiled new D.C. Stadium (later renamed RFK Stadium after Robert Kennedy) on Oct. 1, 1961, for a game against the New York Giants. They built a 21–0 lead, but wound up losing, 24–21.

In 1966 the Redskins and Giants combined to score the most points in any NFL game in Washington's 72–41 victory. The following season, Sonny Jurgensen set an NFL single-season record (since broken) with 3,747 yards passing. Receivers Charley Taylor, Jerry Smith and Bobby Mitchell finished first, second and fourth in the league in receptions.

Vince Lombardi, who had retired as coach of the Green Bay Packers after the 1967 season, took over the Redskins in 1969. Lombardi got immediate results, coaxing a 7–5–2 record out of the Redskins, but died before the next season began. Bill Austin coached the team in 1970, then George Allen was hired. Collecting veteran players from around the league, Allen led the Redskins to a 9–4–1 record and into the playoffs in 1971. For that, he was named the NFL Coach of the Year and forever will be remembered for his quote, "The future is now."

In 1975 Taylor became the NFL leader for career receptions, since broken by Washington's Art Monk.

Jack Pardee took over as head coach in 1978 and won half of his games over the next three seasons. He was replaced by Joe Gibbs in 1981. The Redskins were 8–8 in Gibbs' first season, but in 1982, a strike-shortened season, Washington won Super Bowl XVII over the Miami Dolphins, 27–17. The Redskins were back in the Super Bowl the following year, but lost to the Los Angeles Raiders, 38–9. That season the Redskins and Packers teamed up in maybe the greatest Monday Night Football game in history. The Redskins lost, 48–47, but the teams combined for more than 1,000 yards of offense.

The Redskins were back in the Super Bowl in 1987 and beat the Denver Broncos, 42–10. Washington scored five touchdowns in the second quarter, needing just 18 plays to do it. Quarterback Doug Williams, the first African-American quarterback to start a Super Bowl, was the game's Most Valuable Player. The Redskins won the Super Bowl again in 1991 behind their "Hogs," the affectionate nickname given their offensive line. The running game and quarterback Mark Rypien combined to overpower the Buffalo Bills, 37–24.

Gibbs, whose teams were 140–65 in his 12 seasons as head coach, retired following the 1993 season, and gave way to defensive coordinator and longtime assistant Richie Pettibon. The Redskins were just 4–12 in 1993, the worst record for the club since 1963, and Pettibon was replaced by Norv Turner.

Washington sank even lower in 1994, dropping to 3–13. The Redskins improved to 6–10 in 1995 and 9–7 in '96. They were 8–7–1 in 1997, following the death of longtime owner Jack Kent Cooke. The Redskins' new 78,000-seat stadium in Prince George's County is named in his honor.

*Gus Frerotte has thrown just 41 interceptions in 1,368 pass attempts.*

## INDIVIDUAL RECORDS

### Career

Rushing Yards:  7,472, John Riggins, 1976–79, 1981–85

Passing Yards:  25,206, Joe Theismann, 1974–85

Receptions:  888, Art Monk, 1980–93

Interceptions:  44, Darrell Green, 1983–97

Touchdowns:  90, Charley Taylor, 1964–77

Points:  1,206, Mark Moseley, 1974–86

### Season

Rushing Yards:  1,353, Terry Allen, 1996

Passing Yards:  4,109, Jay Schroeder, 1986

Receptions:  106, Art Monk, 1984

Interceptions:  13, Dan Sandifer, 1948

Touchdowns:  24, John Riggins, 1983

Points:  161, Mark Moseley, 1983

## ACROSS

1. Aide

7. Foe

11. Jamie Asher's position (init.)

12. Auburn T ___ Russell

14. Redskins' career passing leader

18. Tied for the Redskins lead with 4 interceptions in '97

22. Wire service

23. ___ Louis

24. Redskins' career rushing leader

26. West Coast foe (init.)

28. In his debut game in '94 was named NFC Offensive Player of the Week

30. Stadium signage

31. Sass

32. Usual game day (abbr.)

34. Do the Redskins play in Jack Kent Cooke Stadium?

35. 6-pointer (abbr.)

37. Injure

38. Sean Gilbert's position (init.)

39. Contests

41. Ball prop

43. WR signed with Redskins in '94 after 11 years with the Rams

45. Former

46. Redskins' career TD leader

49. Tackles, guards and center (init.)

50. A cheer
52. Hall of Fame QB was Redskins coach from 1966–68
53. Rival pro league (init.)
54. Yea!
56. Redskins' career scoring leader
57. Iron
58. Knot
59. Block from behind
64. Former head coach Casey or T Simmons
65. ___ or die

## DOWN

2. Pull the ball away
3. WR
4. Worthless matter
5. Stomach muscle (abbr.)
6. Allen: The future is ___!
8. Exhibition: ___-season game
9. '60s war site
10. Heavy blocker
13. Shar Pourdanesh's position (init.)
15. LB led Redskins with 9.5 sacks in '97
16. Play back
17. New Mexico TE Walt ___
18. His 17 TDs as senior at Auburn tied Bo Jackson for school record
19. Hall of Fame LB from West Virginia
20. Originally a 9th round pick of

Minnesota, led Redskins in rushing from 1995–97
21. Away
23. Sold out crowd (init.)
25. Playing surface
27. Expectorates
29. Redskins' head coach
33. On the back of a jersey
35. Part of the foot that kicks a ball
36. Roaming DB
37. Column heading on roster (abbr.)
39. Redskins' career interceptions leader
40. Slingin' Sammy
41. 6-pointer (abbr.)
42. Redskins' starting QB from 1989–93
44. His name is on the championship trophy
46. Stop play (init.)
47. Eyes
48. Point value of FG
50. Contests
51. Pick up a loose ball (init.)
55. Won 69 games from 1971–77
58. Deflect
60. Qtr.
61. 1st word of the national anthem
62. Logo registration (abbr.)
63. TV talk: ___, Mom!
65. ___ or die

*Solution on page 196*

## RETIRED UNIFORM NUMBER

Sammy Baugh—33

```
R  A  C  A  E  B  R  E  H  C  S  I  F  J  H
O  O  L  R  N  E  I  P  Y  R  C  T  N  O  A
U  A  W  L  T  S  B  A  U  G  H  R  C  R  U
G  T  P  E  E  O  C  N  E  R  R  A  W  S  S
R  N  U  H  N  N  A  M  E  L  O  C  N  N  S
E  E  L  A  I  S  F  R  A  R  E  I  W  T  N
E  O  L  P  E  M  M  R  E  B  D  T  O  R  E
N  D  E  U  R  A  T  I  U  E  E  S  R  E  S
K  A  H  O  L  I  M  T  T  N  R  O  B  G  N
N  U  C  T  T  L  Z  A  E  H  L  B  Z  Y  E
O  E  T  V  R  L  I  C  N  Y  A  N  A  E  G
M  R  I  G  G  I  N  S  A  N  E  U  R  L  R
R  L  M  M  E  W  E  T  C  T  H  O  O  N  U
N  I  B  D  S  M  O  S  E  L  E  Y  N  A  J
L  S  N  N  A  M  S  I  E  H  T  V  E  M  C
```

| ALLEN | HAUSS | RIGGINS |
|-------|-------|---------|
| BAUGH | JURGENSEN | RYPIEN |
| BOSTIC | MANLEY | SCHROEDER |
| BROWN | MANN | SMITH |
| BUTZ | MITCHELL | TAYLOR |
| COLEMAN | MONK | THEISMANN |
| FISCHER | MOSELEY | WARREN |
| GREEN | OWENS | WILLIAMS |

# CROSSWORD SOLUTIONS

## ARIZONA CARDINALS

## ATLANTA FALCONS

## BALTIMORE RAVENS

## BUFFALO BILLS

## CAROLINA PANTHERS

## CHICAGO BEARS

## CINCINNATI BENGALS

## DALLAS COWBOYS

## DENVER BRONCOS

## DETROIT LIONS

## GREEN BAY PACKERS

## INDIANAPOLIS COLTS

## JACKSONVILLE JAGUARS

## KANSAS CITY CHIEFS

## MIAMI DOLPHINS

## MINNESOTA VIKINGS

## NEW ENGLAND PATRIOTS

## NEW ORLEANS SAINTS

## NEW YORK GIANTS

## NEW YORK JETS

## OAKLAND RAIDERS

## PHILADELPHIA EAGLES

## PITTSBURGH STEELERS

## SAN DIEGO CHARGERS

## SAN FRANCISCO 49ERS

## SEATTLE SEAHAWKS

## ST. LOUIS RAMS

## TAMPA BAY BUCCANEERS

## TENNESSEE OILERS

## WASHINGTON REDSKINS